Aubyn Bernard Rochfort Trevor-Battye

Pictures in prose of nature, wild sport and humble life

Aubyn Bernard Rochfort Trevor-Battye

Pictures in prose of nature, wild sport and humble life

ISBN/EAN: 9783742899569

Manufactured in Europe, USA, Canada, Australia, Japa

Cover: Foto ©ninafisch / pixelio.de

Manufactured and distributed by brebook publishing software (www.brebook.com)

Aubyn Bernard Rochfort Trevor-Battye

Pictures in prose of nature, wild sport and humble life

PICTURES IN PROSE

OF

NATURE, WILD SPORT, AND HUMBLE LIFE

BY

AUBYN TREVOR-BATTYE, B.A.
F.L.S., F.Z.S.
MEMBER OF THE BRITISH ORNITHOLOGISTS' UNION

LONDON
LONGMANS, GREEN AND CO.
AND NEW YORK: 15 EAST 16th STREET
1894

To

MY EARLIEST TEACHER IN NATURAL HISTORY

My Mother

    The voice that led me at the first
      To follow Nature where she moved
    In lips of orchis lightly pursed,
      Or ripples that the swallow loved;

    In jewelled web, in glittered sky,
      In painted poppy princely raised,
    In flashings of the dragon-fly,
      Rings yet its music. God be praised.

    Then this, dear Lady (this that brings
      No reasoned lore, and erudite,
    Nor any deep imaginings,
      But only picture-touches—light

    As songs of summer tossed about
      From forest breath to forest breath—
    Of gentle peoples playing out
      The fateful round of life and death)

    This, Lady, on thy birthday take,
      And love a little shall achieve
    For all the gracious days that make
      The radiance of a golden eve.

PREFACE

THIS book goes out with no other pretensions beyond an aim at accuracy and truth.

The ways of some wild creatures, followed now through many years, are here dropped back into their proper places, so to say, as readably as I can contrive to do it. I have tried not barely to catalogue facts as facts, but to mirror something of the many-sided life of Nature where it beats through the seasons in this and other lands. I have tried, too, to keep touch with an influence there is out of doors, comparable with that of the beautiful in Art, but deeper-reaching, wider, finer—a star for a crimson lamp.

If in this I had perfectly succeeded, he who read would be for that time "in league with the stones of the field," the wind moving in the grasses, the sun playing on his face. And as this cannot be, I am content to hope that here may be found a pleasant companion, to be carried perhaps in the fishing-basket or read by the winter fire.

And yet I am sure that there must be mistakes in it. Perhaps many. It is only after long and patient watching that one can at all venture to generalise from the things one sees. Often, too, the results arrived at one day seem clean contradicted the next. But this is good for every one, if only because it tends to foster that attitude by which alone is learning possible. So that no wise man will be self-satisfied the more because he seems to see anything clearly, whether a law of the universe or a secret of the humble-bee.

Quite distinct from this is the rewarding delight in learning some new truth, and such consolation for imperfect vision as may be cozened out of that old saying, "In the kingdom of the blind the one-eyed is king."

CONTENTS

	PAGE
WITH CARL OF THE HILL	1
THREE FISH	49
MEMORIES	69
A CHILD OF THE PEOPLE	93
CANVEY ISLAND	101
IN THE LAND OF THE GREAT SPIRIT	113
IN NORFOLK BY THE SEA	155
THE WITCH IN KENT	175
OXFORD: THE UPPER RIVER	189
UPON A DAY	207
THE PROCESSION OF SPRING	227
VESPER	245

ADVERTISEMENT

WHERE it has seemed well for the sake of clearness to add scientific names, they are put in footnotes. In these cases the names of the British birds are those in the Ibis list: of the British plants those in Bentham and Hooker's "Flora."

I take leave to thank the proprietors of "Longman's Magazine" and of the "Saturday Review" for permission to reproduce such of these papers as originally appeared in those publications, though in slightly different form.

Also I gratefully acknowledge the kind help of my friend, Mr. W. H. A. Cowell, in the revision of these pages.

›
WITH CARL OF THE HILL

WITH CARL OF THE HILL

A Sketch from Life.

Carl.

In the very heart of Scandinavia lies a great forest. In this forest is a clearing; in the clearing a hut; and here—hunter, farmer, timber-cutter—here lives Carl of the Hill.

Carl's little holding is of so simple a kind you would scarcely know it for a farm. Here are no rows of yellow corn-stacks, no comfortable range of well-tiled buildings, no stockyards knee-deep in sweet straw-litter, none of the signs of well-to-do circumstances that mark an English homestead. The log-made hut has only three compartments—dairy, living-room, and bedroom. Outside, in a sort of compound, is a cow-byre, a stable for the two horses, a wooden frame on which elk-skins are stretched and dried, and a pit covered with boards and rubbish contrived to keep the potatoes from the frost and to hold the store of aspen branches which serve as winter feed for a few black sheep.

Carl's family consists of his wife and seven boys—the youngest but a baby, the eldest a lad of about nineteen. Physically Carl is the perfection of a type not uncommon among the forest Swedes. Tall, broad-shouldered, and deep-chested—lean in the flank but perfectly proportioned—his athletic frame betrays in every shift of poise and movement a daily training to deeds of activity in the open air. His also are the light blue eyes of his fathers, the old Norse. One is struck at once by a remarkable difference between his moustache and hair—the first tawny, the second silvery white. It is not a handsome face, but a fine face—quiet and strong.

Carl never laughs, though this you find out but slowly because of a certain sunniness that clothes the man. It rings in his voice, it is echoed in his footstep, it plays about his keen blue eyes. Better than this, his eyes shine with lovelight (a beautiful old word)—the light of an exceeding kindness for all fellow-things, strongest perhaps towards childhood and old age, towards everything that is weaker and more helpless than himself. And now and then, looking at Carl, you are aware of an expression that is harder to define. It is wistful, it is concentrated, it is a touch more spiritual than the look of every day—the look as of one who sees again an object that holds all his heart, passed now beyond the range of voices or response, beyond the ægis of his tenderness and care. So guessing you would not be wrong. But wait.

One is not prepared to find fine feelings in a squatter in a forest waste? No? Well, at any rate there is Carl of the Hill—Karl-i-berg, as the people call him—who will be our host and our companion for the next few days.

It is already sunset, and there is much to be done before bedtime. The two yoke of steers who have been loose in the little meadow since they finished driving oats must be housed for the night. The black sheep must be brought from the forest into the little compound. The horses have to be rubbed and littered down, the drying elk-skins stretched and turned, and what with one thing and another the evening is well on before, supper over, we are talking in front of the big pine fire, the wife busy with household offices, the small boys in the background swinging bare legs over the sides of their little wooden cribs and listening heart and eyes, and the baby fast asleep. Carl has heard of the moose, though he has, of course, never seen one (he has never left his own country), and in all that can be said about its habits and the ways of hunting it, his interest is prodigious.

Of what did we not talk that night? Of birds and beasts and flowers, of skiddor *versus* Indian snow-shoes, of ways of life in this and other lands.

"Sleep well," said Carl as he bid me good-night; "remember, to-morrow we hunt the elk."

As if I was likely to forget it.

The Elk.

How big the forest is one cannot say. For days a man may wander there and never see its outer rim. There are no roads—none, that is, except here and there a cart-track cleared between the trees.

The elk is not a mountain creature; his part of the forest, taken as a whole, is flat, lying round about the risings of the sudden hills.

We are out this morning, September 17th, just in time to see the sunrise at a quarter to six. "An elk," says Carl, "must be killed to-day, for it is the last day of the season, and we shall want this winter all the food we can get." The reports about wolves, the movements of waterfowl, the early flocking of northern birds, the brilliance of the rowan berries—on signs like these he grounds his belief.

Carl, his preparations over, finds me awaiting him in the opening of one of the little forest paths that radiate from the clearing. "Not that way," he says, "I do not go that way." He spoke these words with a shiver as of cold; I did not know it until afterwards for the involuntary shudder of a sudden pain.

The left barrel of Carl's gun is rifled for an express bullet; the right may be used either as a 16-bore shot gun or for a spherical ball, "because," as he says, "sometimes you can get fairly close to your elk and then the big bullet is best." My own rifle is a 450 Express. Carl takes old Rappe in a lead, while the young dog, Tålle, is entrusted to me. Rappe, the best elk-hound to-day in the centre of Sweden, won a reputation in the forests of Norrland that still keeps his memory green. In a land where a man's life hangs on the intelligence of his dog, the dog that is *perfect* is never bought or sold, for it cannot be valued in terms of money. But it chanced on a day that the old Lapp, Rappe's master, overreached himself in schemes and cunning, and Rappe passed to Carl in payment of a debt; and Rappe in that kind companionship does not regret the change, and, without Rappe, Carl would not be Carl. A really good dog is born, not made; and during Rappe's lifetime, Carl has tried more dogs than he can count, till at length the days brought Tålle, son of Rappe, a wonderful young dog, steady, observant, and wise, only just—not Rappe himself.

For perhaps two hours we walk twenty yards or so apart, keeping chiefly to the paths of the forest creatures which for long distances tend in a given direction following the lie of the land. The sun is behind us, in our faces the breeze. Silence is imperative—one never knows how near an elk may lie. We have seen already many signs of elk—old slots, broken branches, beds where they have lately lain—but nothing fresh. But now Tålle begins to pull on the lead. He is picking something along through the scrub, and I whistle Carl to my side. As soon as we reach soft ground we can see plainly enough the footprints of an elk—of a small one only, and we want no cows nor calves. Tålle, young and eager, is straining on the lead, but Rappe—after one good examinatiou, nose and eyes—looks up to Carl for orders, for he has sampled that elk to a fraction; he will go if he is bidden, but clearly does not ask to go.

Old Rappe, you are right. So, still with the dogs

in hand, we move quietly on. And now it is Rappe's turn. Carefully we follow Rappe, as, nose down, he takes us through a patch of blaeberries and down to the edge of a moss, and lo! before us is the slot of a big bull, leading right across the moss. Rappe looks up into his master's face as who should say, "It is right enough this time, come along." I was fairly astonished. The trail was clearly at least twenty hours old—such a trail as no moose-hunter would have looked at twice; but then we do not use dogs when we follow the moose. So we go on, slowly at first, but with a gradually mending scent, until at last we are fairly running. It is quite difficult in that rough ground to keep one's feet, for both the hounds, though mute, are pulling all they know. After some time at this we come suddenly on a bed among some rushes where the elk has lain. Beyond this point the track is fresh, and then we slip the hounds and stand in silence, waiting what shall fall. I look at my watch—it is one o'clock.

Presently the deep tongue of Rappe is brought back upon the wind with Tålle's higher voice. "Elgen" (the elk) says Carl below his breath; and then we follow on.

Now an elk, in an ordinary way, will not pay much attention to a well-trained dog. He will just move slowly along, stopping now and then, as he finds the dog in front, to butt, or strike at it with his feet. For a good dog never bites or hurries the elk; his duty is only to try and engage its attention till the hunter comes up. Nor does the woodman's axe, the noise of a fowling-piece, nor any sight or sound of every day alarm the elk. It is only when, putting two and two together, he concludes that man is after *him* that he is really startled and then —he goes! When that happens the hounds return at once to the hunter, for a frightened elk will go for thirty miles or more at a swinging trot, taking timber in his stride and even crossing lakes.

Our elk is not exactly startled, but he is uneasy. He has probably been hunted before; so he keeps drawing away and drawing away, and still the day wears on.

A stern chase is a long chase, and though we might have shot the elk earlier but for the denseness of the trees, it is not till late in the afternoon that, turning the corner of a small watercourse, we come upon him standing knee-deep in the stream, perhaps eighty yards away. It is a fine sight. For all his quaint old-world appearance, he seems wonderfully fitted to his actual surroundings, as indeed every wild animal always does. Born of the forest, it is his beyond all challenge: his cradle, his birthright, his realm. So there he stands in the majesty of his size and strength, lowering at intervals a scornful head to meet the feints and shiftings of his tireless foes. Lightly flows the tinkling streamlet by moss and boulder down to his feet; and away behind him stretches the narrow glen in yellow of aspen, and scarlet of maple, and sombre background of the mournful pine. A beautiful sight indeed, one to linger over and to dream about. But we are here not to look at pictures but to get the winter's food. So the elk must fall, and fall he does, but not before he has travelled halfway up the glen with a ball in the shoulder and a second in the withers, and then, receiving Carl's big bullet behind the ear, he pitches head first against a boulder and so he lies.

"Now," said Carl, "we must gralloch this animal, then make our way back as well as we can, and to-morrow we will bring the sleigh." No sooner were the words out of his mouth than the same thought struck us both. For there was a rumour that wolves had been seen in the district.* So it was agreed that I should remain to do the gralloching and mount guard over the slain, while Carl made the best of his way back to the clearing, and tomorrow he would come with the sleigh. But the elk had fallen in an awkward position. Carl therefore helped me to turn him about; and not until I saw him handling the colossal creature that had stood at the shoulder all sixteen hands, not till then had I realised Carl's prodigious strength. And so Carl left; and with him went Rappe the wise and faithful, while Tålle, at his master's bidding, stayed with me.

It did not take long to gralloch the elk, and then it was time to think of supper. Fortunately I was not doomed to eat a tough elk-steak, for Tålle, who while elk was in the wind had kept strictly to business, now condescended to tree for me a hjerpe or hazel grouse. I was afraid of smashing it with an expanding bullet, but was lucky enough to blow off its head, so that my supper did not lose. The bird, plucked and stuffed with elk-fat,

---

* I feel pretty certain now that this rumour was incorrect. The fact that one stray wolf had been killed there the previous winter proves nothing. Thirty years ago wolves were not infrequently found in severe winters as far down even as

was soon swinging before a pine-wood fire at the end of Tålle's lead. The result, at any rate, was food; and after groping a dessert of lingen and blaeberries I felt that I could last it out.

So presently, tumbling down a boulder from under the overhanging branches of a pine-tree, I lined the hollow with ferns and brushwood and made a bed like the nide of a bear; remembering the name I had borne among the Crees—Mcquah, "the Bear"—because of this habit which I had. For a Red Indian on the hunt will prepare no bed, but squats over his fire all through the night. But I knocked my fire to pieces, hoping that the wolves would come. For a long time I lay there, listening to the night voices and waiting for a shot. There was no moon, but it was a perfect night. High up in the heavens hung Jupiter, a silver globe, and lower down burnt Mars the lurid just above a line of pines. And a tide of trembling stars seemed to gather up to roof the span above me, closing in the glen to its very fringe as though it were the sanctuary of the world.

Scåne. But now, speaking generally, the wolf is extinct in the centre of Sweden, though wolves had really appeared early in September 1892 on the fjells near Roraas, across the border.

I had plenty of time for marvel and reflection, for, though my rifle was ready to cover the hollow below me, no wolves came. Once I fancied I could catch a long-drawn howl upon the night wind, and once it seemed that Tålle turned and growled; but whether I was awake or sleeping then I could not say, for the next thing I knew was that the sun was showing between the maples and the forest was ringing like a cathedral choir.

Carl had twenty miles to go and come, and he did not arrive with the grey horse and the sleigh (wheels are useless in that rough country) till the middle of the day. Then we loaded the elk's big carcass, and after a difficult and devious journey reached the clearing at the fall of night.

The Säter in the Hill.

Now as I write these words in England, on the 17th of November, the sparrows, stirred by a sunshiny morning, are busy above my window building hard at their nests. And many birds, as any one may notice, repeat in a fine autumn the love-passages of the spring. The capercaillie or tjeder does so, and according to Carl it is his almost daily practice between September 15th and the end of the month. At these times this great bird, usually so shy and difficult of approach, may be secured with comparative ease when engaged in his grotesque exercises. And one of the best grounds for tjeder in these parts is Carl's hill—or perhaps it would call itself a mountain, for it is about two thousand feet high. Over this hill Carl, because of his timber dealings, has all the forest rights; and as business was taking him up that way he proposed that I should go with him. I would go anywhere where Carl would take me, but I was the more inclined to the project because I should then see the rock on which a pair of eagle owls breed every season, and possibly see the birds themselves. I should also have time to study the ways of the crested titmouse, whose acquaintance I had made in Spain. So it was arranged that we should start the following morning, taking Nora, the brown mare, in the four-wheeled cariole, and working on by forest ways till we hit the landvagen or high road, should follow this up and reach the home of a friend of Carl where the cariole might wait.

Then we went by the winding roads of the forest, shooting what we could and stopping often to observe the ways of things about, till we came out at last on the landvagen, one of the wildest roads and certainly the worst that ever presumed upon the distinction "high.' And after much tough work on the collar we found high up a little cluster of wooden houses, grouped about one of greater pretensions with a flagstaff and a store. The holder of all this vested interest was Olaf Christen*sen*, as he took the trouble to make it clear. A Dane by birth and rotund by training, he had originally been a whaler in the Arctic seas. But, induced by the profits of two good seasons, he had exchanged his boat for an inland store; and, still retaining some interest in the seal and blubber line, had come to be a considerable person in those parts. He was busy taking to pieces an *al fresco* platform hung with evergreens and gaily decked about, for there had lately been a wedding and festal doings and much dancing of the lads and girls.

But as soon as Carl appeared, all work was dropped. From all sides the neighbours gathered in, and great was the health-drinking, hand-shaking, hugging, and doffing of hats. The enthusiasm of old Olaf at meeting an Englishman was beyond all holding. Yes, yes, he had been to England, he told me, though that was long ago. It afterwards turned out that this referred to a visit to the Kyle of Tongue, in which, driven by a storm, he had lain three days. But time was pressing, and we had hard work to get away. We only escaped at last under promise to come on our return to a feast, that "Engelsman" might see that the Swedes were his friends, and that Carl might relate his adventures since last he was that way.

From this point, then, we struck on foot into the forest where it was settled up in parts; and the wonders of that eventful journey I have no space to tell. It was like moving through a fairy story, so aptly things fell out. Whether Carl had really contrived to send a herald on I never could make sure; for when I asked him he only smiled and answered that "in all savage countries news travelled very fast." But in one house the floor had been strewn with fresh spruce branches, and coffee-berries had just been roasted on the hearth. The mother gave us a cheery welcome, but the daughter only smiled from the corner a blushing greeting and would not leave her wheel. And I remembered how I had said to Carl, that I hoped I should see some spinning, for that in our own country it was dying out. And once we came in sight of a mountain lake and I wondered how we should cross it. And lo! as we got nearer, an old man was waiting in a queer crank boat and took us in. Very silently he rowed us, I remember, and with head bent down, as though he were sad at heart or pondering many things. At another point out ran some bare-footed children to give us bunches of sweet Linnæa which they had found in flower in some warm corner among the pines, crying, "Linnæa, Linnæa," as they came along. And though I had seen much of this plant I had never seen as yet the flower, which only blossoms fully in the early summer, though afterwards I saw it many times. And about that small, sweet, bell-like flower there is a little story, so pretty as it seems to me that, even if well known and whether true or untrue, I must tell it here.

Old Linnæus lay upon his death-bed. The winner of secrets, the magician of nature, the reformer of science would soon have passed away. All that he had brought to the information of the centuries and the equipment of his age would be a memory and no more. Now true greatness is ever humble, and Carolus Linnæus was truly great. And so it had come about that he had connected his name with not one of his many discoveries, being only concerned with the one thing—Truth. But his friends, jealous for his honour and mindful of how short is the memory of the world, prayed him that he would let his name be given to which ever one of his discoveries himself had valued most. And then the old man raised himself to say in his sweet simpleness, "There is the little northern plant, long neglected, trailing low, that blooms with downward petals in the early year. Let it then be this." So *Linnæa borealis* the plant was named. And alone of all wild plants it has no local other name; for as Linnæa it is known alike to the learned and to the cottage children wherever it grows.

But now we had passed the last small settlement and were fairly up among the hills. Not very fast did we travel, however, for on the way we hunted hares till one of the dogs fell badly lame. This in its turn again delayed us, so that we did not reach the point of our wanderings till the sun had set and night was closing in.

The spot where we found ourselves was a grass patch some fifteen hundred feet up on the side of a conical hill. On this patch were four buildings—two were cow-byres, two were säters. One of the säters was closed and deserted, as you might see by the big stone that covered the top of the chimney, the other had a fire burning inside.

It may interest those who only know Norway, to hear what a säter in the Swedish hills is like; for they are all of a pattern and a size. Built of rough-hewn pine-trees, the cracks filled in with daub and heather, their outside measurement is perhaps eighteen feet by twelve. There are two compartments; in front the living-room, behind the dairy. There are no windows, properly so called; just a little hole on either side screened by a movable board. Round the room runs a wooden settle on which the occupants sleep and sit. In the corner of the door is the big hearth, over which hangs a large projecting hood, all built of stone and plastered in, up which there is perfect ventilation through the low, wide chimney, so that the air in a säter is always fresh. But uncomfortable place as it may appear from this description, it is not really so. With its floor bespread with sweet shoots of the fir-tree, with the red light of the fire twinkling on the polished surfaces of the copper vessels that hang around, and lighting up the kind honest faces of its homely occupants, it is not uncomfortable then.

During the summer months the cattle are sent

from the farms in the valleys up to the mountains to feed. Each small herd is in charge of its dairywoman, and for her the säter is built. It is lonely enough during the week, but on Saturdays and Sundays their friends come up to see them, so that, what with this and their knitting and dairy work, they get along pretty well. Now September the 19th is the day on which the mountain feeding is over and the cows return to the farms. One of the women had therefore left that very morning, but the other, as if apprised of Carl's coming, would seem to have agreed to remain till the Monday to give him welcome and see to his wants. And yet when we entered the säter its only occupant was a man. A lazy sullen-looking fellow he was, who informed us that he had come up to see his sister, but that at present she was out.

Now, as we found out later, it was out of no love for his sister that he was there, but because he had arranged to meet a companion at this place and do a bit of poaching on Carl's ground. Owing, however, as I imagine to the scent of Carl's coming, this precious plan fell through. He told us, then, that his sister had only that evening discovered that her cows had followed the others in the morning when they left. The girl would therefore have to trudge a Swedish mile and a half (about ten English miles) till she reached the neighbour's farm—it lay in the opposite valley—and then, unaided and alone, bring the cattle back through the lonely forest at night.

"And why did you not go instead of her?" asked Carl; "were you not ashamed to let a woman take that journey and you sitting idling here?" "They ain't *my* cows," was all the answer the man vouchsafed. "Well, you had better go after her now," said Carl. The man replied that he did not know which way she had gone. There was a dangerous glitter in Carl's blue eyes, but he only said, and very quietly, "Then you had better go and find out." But the man, deceived perhaps by the calmness of Carl's voice, made no response. "You had better go and find out," repeated Carl in just the same slow measured tones. And still the man moved not. And then up rose Carl, and in one stride had crossed the room. And before the other had realised what was coming, a huge right hand had closed about his neck. And so, feet trailing on the floor, Carl bore him, lifting the latch with his free left hand, and out through the doorway and on to the little potato patch in front And there he dropped him, saying as he did so, in the same dispassioned tones, "You had better go and find out," and so returned to the house in the quiet good temper of every day. The man appeared no more that night nor thereafter so long as we remained: but at three o'clock the following morning, I, who had crept out to look at the wonder of Venus in the heavens which then was flashing like the star of old, saw in a cow-byre a light; and lo! the woman had returned from a forest tramp of twenty miles, and came on to the säter without a sign of weariness, but singing as she came.

It was on the evening after this that Carl took me up to the top of the hill, under solemn promise that I would not look behind until he gave me leave. So we climbed till we came to a huge and jagged boulder that seemed the end of all things; for below it was the vast of mountain and forest, and beyond it was the sky. And then we turned and looked. "There," said Carl; "often when I have been hard at work all day in the forest below, I come up here to look at that, and so I do not feel tired."

And indeed it was a beautiful scene.

Around us lay the cold grey shapes of the lichened boulders, and among them a single dying pine-tree reared its bare gaunt form—the sentry-post of the birds of prey. Below this on a shred of green velvet were the lonely säters and the smoke wreathing up into the amber sky. After this there was nothing rugged, all was very soft. For beyond them three little lakes were lying—steel-blue in the inlets, white under the finger of the shifting breezes, red in the eye of the sun. And again one caught the glitter of winding water in the passes and the hollows of the hills. On the left the scene rose to a sublimer beauty—in line upon line of pine-fringed ridges, piled as the steps to a stupendous temple, till they lost themselves in the summit called the Cap of Odin, cold cut against the eastern sky.

The day following we left the säter, and after the promised feast at Olaf Christensen's, started with the cariole for the drive home. It was a drive I shall never forget.

Nora was a very fast and very beautiful Norwegian mare, with a mouth of iron, and the temper of a fiend. As she was a confirmed kicker and bolter Carl had bought her for a song, for, as her owner was wont to say, "It was only a question of time—and she would kill a man some day." And this was the animal we were to sit behind, going back to her stable on a down-hill journey with a two days' rest and her belly full of corn.

I am free to admit that it was not without a feeling of concern that I noticed Carl starting on the journey, the reins lying loose on Nora's back. During the whole of that long distance Carl never once took a pull at the mare's mouth, nor do I remember that he ever once so much as stirred the reins except when we had to turn to right or left. Then he would just raise a rein, letting it fall again on the creature's back. And little time had he to bestow on any remarks of mine, for he was talking almost continually to Nora in a low voice as we went along. And the mare as if stirred by the magic of sympathy would shake her pretty head, and seem to answer every word. And sometimes when, getting beyond herself, she would begin to reach out and extend herself into a slashing stride, Carl would only say in his quiet accents, "Gently, Nora; gently, you dear Nora." And then the mare would drop back into paces self-contained, though the sweat was streaming down her flanks and she shook her bridle till the foam flew again.

There are some things that stand out above all others when I look back on those days with Carl of the Hill. I remember the first sight of the clearing in the forest, I remember the elk-hunt, I remember the wonderful drive. But oftenest I recall that evening on the hill above the säter, for there Carl told me the story of Little Sunlight that follows hereupon. There are sorrows that are too sacred for words. There are sorrows which a man must carry in his own consciousness and none else may know them in this life. But there are also times when men are thrown together under the compelling influence of a great danger, or the divine touch of a beautiful solitude— when, for league upon league of distance, and between them and the circling horizon, there is no other human life, only they two of all the world—and then the heart will speak.

Very simply and beautifully Carl told his story and in far fewer words than I. But I must tell it as I may be able, since I cannot tell it in Carl's way.

Carl did not seem to be telling a story, he seemed only as a man *remembering aloud*. And often his voice would sink to accents so quiet and contemplative I had much ado to gather what he said. And sometimes he paused for long together, and in those silences I could glance up at his face. And upon it was the wistfulness I have spoken of before. And he ended very gently, but with a face so rapt and so illuminated he was as one who was conscious of no earthly thing that lies within his range of vision, but sees beyond the golden doors of the sunset, beyond the bourne of the spangled stars, where children play in the gardens of the morning that never grows to noon or night.

Such is the power of love.

The Story of Little Sunlight.

Carl, as I said before, is by profession a timber merchant, or more correctly a lumberer. He also does a trade in furs. There is no more practised hunter and trapper in all the district round than he, no man more versed in all the detail of device for taking wild things, from the horsehair noose at the end of a bender to the heavy log which, propped up across a forest track, is known as the dead-fall trap. But this form of trap he does not like, and has not set at all during the last few years.

To say that Carl is a naturalist is to speak but half the truth. Say rather that he is a very priest of nature. It is not only that he knows the names and life-history of every flower and bird about him—oh yes, he knows that; they are his friends and his companions, and as such he loves them—but it is more. It is as though Nature, the Great Mother, has commissioned him her own. No breath that comes from the gates of the morning but brings to him its message from her throne; no star that looks over the top of the mountains but tells him something wonderful and new. The falling leaf, the rushing stream, the mist that writhes over the mosses at evening, speak straight to him in accents that he knows.

Carl's father was the penniless pastor of a neighbouring cure. Having educated his boy in the High School and finished him off at the University of Upsala, he married him at the age of nineteen to the only child of a Carlstad timber merchant. He felt then that he had done his duty, and preached the next Sunday with fuller grace.

Carl himself raised no objection. The girl was pretty, he loved her, and loved a forest life. But her father, who had not been consulted, and had always schemed that she should marry the Jägmästare, was beside himself with rage. He vowed that if any man thought he was going to get money by marrying *his* daughter he was very much mistaken. All of which was fair enough. However, he had sufficient penetration to be conscious of Carl's worth and made him foreman and manager in the forest. By-and-by he relented somewhat: and presently—having made a will in which he left to Carl the farm-holding with certain forest rights, but every penny of capital to a second wife—he died happy.

Carl's wife, who was older than himself, very soon lost her good looks. She was a stupid, badly educated woman, though a good and dutiful wife. She understood the art of making cheese and butter, was very handy with her needle, and bore Carl four sons who would be useful on the farm some day. All these things she did very well. She knew nothing of the difference between her husband and herself—indeed, she could not have understood it, and therefore could not know. As for Carl, he was never impatient with her, and never wronged her by word or thought.

He was fond of his boys and worked hard at trying to educate them. But they, unfortunately, seemed to have their mother's want of wits and were not companionable as some boys are. And Carl would come home from his work in the beautiful forest, only to be thrown back upon himself as he crossed his threshold by the hopelessness of the commonplace he found inside. And more and more there took shape in his being the demands of a great need that would not be denied. The need of an object of love and sympathy that could exhaust all homage under God, in the absolute abandonment of his strong soul.

At last it came.

It had been a time of gloom and leaden skies. The winter had been no milder than Scandinavian winters usually are. But at length there were signs that spring was not far off. And Carl, who had been hunting northwards, felt it was time to go. There were other reasons, too, which urged him home. So the sleigh was laden with the spoils of Carl's labour, furs of the bear and ermine, of marten and lynx, and he started away over the frozen snow-fields.

South he came till he passed by Siljan, where in summer the wild swans nest. It was a long and lonely journey, and it took much time; but at last he reached the head of Fryken and then he felt he was at home. A week later the day broke in a flood of sudden sunshine and spring had come. That morning a little daughter was born to Carl.

They have in Swedish a beautiful old word that means sunshine, or more properly sunlight, and Carl by an instant instinct fixed upon this as the name for the child. The mother did not like it. It was not a fit name for a Christian, she said, and it was so fanciful that every one would laugh. But Carl had his own reasons, though he kept them to himself. He only repeated in his quiet way, "Yes, we will call her Sunlight: it was sunlight when she came." Sunlight therefore the child was called.

Perhaps I need not dwell so lingeringly as Carl upon those early days of little Sunlight's life. Imperial babyhood—its history is one; differing in nothing from that of all autocracies, but in the willing service of its slaves. But for Carl a new vision of life was opened up.

It was not only the interest, which the boys shared with him, in the little helpless presence that seemed to make all gentler in that rude home; it was not even love parental, deep though that was and strong. It was far, far more to Carl.

For Carl of the day-dreams would look beyond the present; beyond even that happy time of her childhood that was coming when he should mould and teach her and give her all he might. He looked over this again into the years that lay beyond when Sunlight should have come to the majesty of maidenhood. He saw her in touch with bird and flower and evening star— the perfect expression of Nature's aim. He saw her beautiful—the crown and music of all that forest's life. She should be an artist, he would think, and the magic of her art should arrest the shifting wonders of lake and sky that his poor blundering hand had sometimes tried to paint. And Carl, who had a poet's soul, had tried at times to shape his utterance into something like an echo of the thoughts that were in him; but—oh yes, he knew it—in such halting numbers. But then there would be no more failures; for hers would be the inspiration, till the world would listen to their song. Further, nothing sorrowed or bewildered Carl more than the mystery of pain and suffering. The spectacle of a being—of a child especially—in distress was always a shock to him as of actual physical pain. He had plenty of room in the little settlements about him for the exercise of a relieving kindness, where simple gratitude welcomed him and blessed his name. But after all he was but a clumsy man—as was often his reproachful reflection; and then he would think of Sunlight moving round in her sweet graciousness, "a voice of comfort, and an open hand of help."

So every day, and earlier than had ever been his wont, the great strong man returned from his labour to rock a cradle with his foot. His wife said little. She was only too glad to find him so domestic, though she took it for a sign that he was beginning to feel old.

So the summer wore to winter and the next spring came and the seasons followed thereupon, and like a flower grew the child. And it seemed, indeed, as if Carl's dream were coming true. Sunlight was now in her eighth year: straight as an arrow, graceful as a deer. Quick as were her instincts and wonderful her loveliness, there was nothing precocious, nothing elfin, about her character or face. The child of nature was she, but in its fairest and breeziest sense. In her the poet's thought seemed realised,

*And beauty born of murmuring sound
Shall pass into her face.*

For it was as though each element in Nature's hand had given her something of itself: the sun her hair, the heaven her eyes, the stream her laughter, and the birds her voice. But better far than all was the child's sweet disposition and her gentle ways of love.

It was wonderful to see how the influence of one little child could radiate even through a district so thinly settled-up as that. Yet so it was Carl's hut became a rallying-point for all the forest round. The Sunday would bring down friends from Olaf's settlement, for all that they had to be back at work by the first thing the following day. Rough wood-cutters would frame any clumsy excuse so they might take Carl's hut on their way from work. And there they would sit without a word to say for themselves, gazing at Sunlight with great foolish faces, happy in her lightest word. Their poor silent homage they gave her as of right: she was their queen, and any one of them would have died for her had there been need.

Carl, in any moments he could snatch from his occupation, would devote himself to the child. And sometimes by doing double work one day he could contrive a holiday the next, and these were Sunlight's festal days. For then she could go with him a whole long day into the forest, and when she was tired he could carry her on his broad shoulder many and many a mile. Under him the forest became to her a palace of living wonders, for he taught her all he knew. He showed her how the speckled spider made its web; and how the dew hung there like gems of light, and why. How, too, the dew was there some mornings, and on others not; the meaning of the rainbow he showed her and why the west grows red. He gave her reasons for all these things; the deep yet simple reasons that there are, though people commonly never trouble their heads about them because they are happening every day. He showed her the best places in which to find Linnæa—where it grew thickest and flowered finest when the spruces were first cut, and he told her why that was. They went to see the stone deep under which the foxes had their litter, and then lay down in the fern with the wind in their faces and watched the little cubs tumbling and rolling one over the other like kittens at their play. They came upon an old fir-tree one day with a big hollow at its roots, and Carl told Sunlight how an old bear had slept there all last winter and that his skin would be ready next winter for the sleigh.

Those were days indeed. And Sunlight, with her cheek against her father's as he strided on, would think that no little girl had ever had such a wonderful father before. And Carl would answer he was quite sure that they all had a wonderful Father who was Carl's Father too. That He had made the beautiful forest and made everything, and why he, Carl, thought it had been made. And that though she could not see Him she must never forget Him, for He saw her always and guided all His children with His eye. He never spoke, He only looked, but then we knew exactly what He wanted, and whether we were doing right or wrong.

Sunlight had a remarkable influence over all dumb creatures. Grålle, the grey horse, who was queer tempered with every one else, would nestle his old muzzle down against her cheek, and Rappe's predecessor, a cross-grained dog, was always gentleness itself with her. Carl had built for the child a sort of bower of spruce fir branches up among the arms of an old pollard near the hut. She called it her castle, and went up and down by a little ladder. Here a red squirrel used to watch her, and watch her with bright black eyes. Each day he would come and look, venturing a little nearer—a little nearer—and Sunlight would keep as still as a mouse, moving not so much as an eyelid. At last his confidence grew so assured that he would come and take bits of mushroom from her fingers, and sit there close with his tail over his back, nibbling the dainty with absolute unconcern. But if one of the boys were in there with her the squirrel would not come. He would give one glance round the corner and, seeing the intruder, hurtle away backwards up the tree in a series of jerks and angry "chucketings," his resentment was so great.

New Year's Eve was a great occasion at the hut. Then Olaf Christensen, Sunlight's godfather, would come down to spend the night, and Sunlight—the one day in all the year—could hear the midnight clock strike twelve. And then they would sing the old hymn that runs—

> *It is gone across the snow,*
>   *All the old year that I knew;*
> *It is gone for weal or woe,*
>   *Good or evil, false or true.*
> *With the new year, Saviour mild,*
> *Make me as a little child;*

and then all would go to bed. But until twelve o'clock they used to sit round the fire, while Carl in his wonderful way was telling sagas. And once as they listened to the story of the Great King Olaf, Sunlight sitting on her father's knee, her head on his shoulder, following half asleep some train of childish thought, broke in suddenly with, "Father, dear, when you get very old will you have white hair like Uncle Olaf's is?" "Uncle" Olaf roared aloud; he did not feel so very old. Carl also laughed and answered, "No, little Sunlight, Uncle Olaf's hair was black, my *yellow* hair will never grow white." Sunlight's face fell at this sudden blow, but she only said resignedly, "Oh, I wanted so to stroke it when you are telling sagas."

Sunlight's birthday came to be a sort of festival in the clearing. It was always kept on the first of June, (though well after the date of the real event) because the weather was sure then to be safe. The Linnæa, too, was well in bloom, and the children could make a wreath of it and crown Sunlight, just as here in England the children crown a Queen of the May.

It was now the last day of May, and to-morrow they would celebrate Sunlight's eighth birthday. Carl's wife went off early in the cariole to buy presents and some stores for the morrow. Carl, who meant to make a double holiday, had promised himself a long day with Sunlight in the forest. But just as they were starting some one arrived to say that one of the men had met with an accident the day before, and was lying in a hut a long way off in the hills and greatly in need of help. Carl at once determined that he must go and see him. He would have taken Sunlight with him but the cariole was gone, so there was nothing for it but to mount the other horse and journey off alone. He consoled Sunlight for her disappointment, saying he should try and be back by the middle of the day, and he left her in the care of her eldest brother, then a lad of about fifteen. The two youngest boys, both much younger than Sunlight, the mother had taken with her.

For a long time the children played about the clearing. They stormed and defended Sunlight's castle and amused themselves in many ways. At last it was proposed that they should play at hunting elk. So the eldest boy went off with a start as the elk, and giving him a few minutes' law, the others presently followed. Sunlight, who was as active as a young roe, had no difficulty in keeping up. But, catching sight of some butterfly or flower, for a few moments she was left behind. When she followed on, she took in her eagerness a wrong turning and soon found that she had lost the boys. This mattered little to her, she knew that part of the forest by heart, and was soon back at the point where the footprints of her brothers showed she had gone wrong. Here, she thought, she would wait till they returned. So she sat and waited. But after a bit, hearing no sound of returning voices, she found her way back to the hut. The boys had not come home.

It was now about the middle of the day, and Sunlight thought she would go and meet her father. So she tripped off across the clearing and took the forest path up which she had seem him ride. It was one of the most beautiful of early summer days, and you may fancy how light the child's heart was. To-morrow would be her birthday, and a splendid time it would be. So singing a little song she went. It was the quaint jingle of a children's game; the children had sung it last year, and would sing it again to-morrow:

> *Where does our lady keep house, I pray?*
> *Out in the forest so pretty and green.*
> *What shall we do when she comes this way?*
> *We'll crown her with flowers and make her our queen.*

And then under an arcade of little joined hands the queen would pass along. That was how the game went, and the tune had been running in Sunlight's head all day. I think that sweet young presence as it came along must have seemed the very genius of that fairy scene. I think even the little stupid lemming must have popped his round head out of the grass tufts wondering at the brightness of this new sunbeam that fell across the path. Yes, Sunlight was very, very happy. Every moment she expected to see her father come riding round a turn in the path, and she laughed as she thought how surprised and pleased he would be to find his little daughter come to meet him; and how he would catch her to the saddle and she would ride with him home.

Presently she found a little bird—a crested titmouse—that had a broken wing. And thinking she would take it home and make it well, she picked it up and held it very gently so as not to hurt its wing.

But Sunlight in reality had wandered much farther than she had ever been before alone. And now, with head bent down, and crooning to the bird, she took, quite unawares, a narrow side track—one of the paths of the forest creatures. And coming to a huge tree limb that crossed the path, one end on the ground, the other reared up among the undergrowth of the opposite side, she stooped beneath it.

Meanwhile the boys had come back to the clearing. They were surprised at first at not finding Sunlight there. And for some little time they ran about looking for her and shouting out her name. But getting no answer they thought she was probably hunting for butterflies or flowers, for she had always been a self-reliant little creature. And as they were hungry they presently had dinner and then went out to play again, forgetting all about her. It was not until the evening was drawing on that they began again to wonder where she was, and then to feel really unhappy.

Carl came back soon after sundown and found his wife was just arrived. "Where was Sunlight?" The boys could not tell him, though they told him all they knew. He thought it very strange, but fancying she might only be hiding in play, or perhaps preparing some pretty surprise for him, he shouted out her name, saying it was getting too late for little girls to be out and that she must come in at once. To all this there was no answer. So then he brought out his hunting-bugle and blew clear and long the supper-time call which the children and the foresters knew quite well. Through the clear air that sound would travel a mile and more; but neither to this—though he waited through an anxious half-hour—was there any response. And then he thought she must be lost, though he could not understand it: she knew the forest for a mile around so well. Though greatly distressed and unhappy he did not feel any terrible anxiety—nothing *could* hurt his little Sunlight; of that he felt quite sure. But still he ate no supper, and taking a lantern, and giving another to his eldest boy, they started in different directions for the search. The lad returned about one o'clock, completely tired out and with nothing to report.

As for Carl, he visited every spot where he thought there was the faintest chance of her having gone. He went to a particular bed of Linnæa, the last and finest he had shown her, where he thought she might have gone to gather flowers for to-morrow's fête. He went to the old aspen-tree where was the nest of the black woodpecker that Sunlight had been watching, as he knew. He went to the stream where the young otters were, and a horrible dread for the first time overtook him as he thought she might have fallen in. He swept the pool with the light of his lantern, and once a terrible cry escaped his lips as he fancied he saw the glimmer of a child's white frock. But it was only the foam where it was caught by the willows, and again he turned to try elsewhere. About two o'clock he returned to the hut to see if there was any news. And hearing "none," he said never a word, but started out again.

So without a moment's pause he hunted till dawn and then a sudden inspiration struck him. *Of course* she had gone to meet him! She had gone by the way he went. With that he flung the lantern down and ran as he had never run before. He reached the entrance to the pathway. There were the marks of his horse's hoofs, and there sure enough were the tracks of the child's footprints leading right on down the path. They were very slight, but plain enough to the practised eye of the hunter. So he went on hunting like a hound: running sometimes, and sometimes, where the ground was hard, picking it along with painful care. Presently in his eagerness he lost the footprints altogether and so stood quite at fault. He harked back. He found the tracks again at the point where a little crooked path left the other, and into it he bounded like a stag. At first he could make out nothing, the ground was so dry and hard. But now he came to a soft and reedy patch, and there sure enough was again the print of a tiny foot. He panted on with redoubled speed and then, all in a moment, he stopped and reeled while the sweat burst in great beads from his forehead. He remembered his dead-fall trap! Nothing, he knew well, that had passed beneath that dropping weight of timber had ever come out alive. He held his hand in front of his eyes with a convulsive clutch. Mastering himself, he went on slowly. He knew the exact turn in the path from which he could get the first glimpse of the trap. Well enough he knew it—had he not often crept up there, all interest, to see what luck was his? He reached that point. Perhaps his head was beginning to go: at any rate he turned his back and laughed. "Impossible! as if any harm could ever come to Sunlight, his darling, his gift from God." And then he began to sing—the first thing that came to his lips:

> *What shall we do when she comes this way?*
> *We will crown her with flowers, and make her our queen.*

How long he stood so no man may say. But at length with a strong effort he swung himself and turned. Then, for one moment, his heart stopped, and, with a terrible crash, he fell and swooned.

They found Carl at last. They helped him to stagger homewards, bearing in his arms the form of little Sunlight, in her left hand a bunch of sweet Linnæa, in her right a little living bird.

But Sunlight was to live no more in the forest. She had gone to the Father of all the children—the Father, too, of Carl.

The grey horse Grålle took Sunlight to her funeral. It had been a very beautiful birthday, though there had been no singing as in other years—none, at least, that mortal ear could hear. Little Sunlight's blue eyes were closed, but on her face was such a smile as seemed to fill the room with light; as though she caught the echo of a children's choir:

We will crown her with flowers, and make her our queen.

The little bird was there. At first the boys had tried to feed it, but could not for their tears. So they just put it by her hands in a fold of the coverlet and there it nestled, looking with bright eyes at the children as they came. For one by one they came and kissed her, and, in the silence, crowned her queen.

Where Carl was no one knew—out in the forest somewhere, anywhere, wrestling with his grief.

The grey horse took Sunlight to her funeral. Above Sunlight's bower the squirrel sat. He had never seen so many flowers on any birthday. Every day he had sat there waiting, and wondering why she did not come with food.

Down the long forest track the train of mourners crept and the neighbours joined it as it went along.

Close behind the cariole walked a man bareheaded, whom none could recognise, though they knew it must be Carl. But it seemed to be the figure of an old, old man, for the broad back was bowed and the hair was snowy white. And men looked at one another with awe-struck faces. "It will kill him," was what they said.

But it did not kill him. For a whole year he was as one dead to every interest of life, hopeless, crushed. And then the time of Sunlight's birthday came round again. For two whole days and nights he was seen of none. Out into the forest he went, and what happened there who can tell? But he came back again with a light in his eyes and a smile upon his features—a man transformed. And from that moment he straightened himself up to take again his part in the common battle of life.

What happened in the forest who can tell? None. But a great love is wonderful in its strength and patience—Carl could wait.

THREE FISH

THREE FISH

THERE is nothing in the trivial facts which follow beyond this. Last night I happened to be putting some tackle together and fell to musing on three fish. These.

Fish the First.

I had been idling at beautiful Monterey on the Pacific Coast, where all day long the humming-birds are glancing about the heliotrope, and the great white fishing pelicans taking headers in the bay. From there I moved up into the Sierra Nevada, to hunt the bear and black-tailed deer.

And one day, 'returned from hunting, I chanced upon an encampment of Digger Indians by the side of a clear running stream. They fed me with fish. Good fish. Trout.*

I was up and down at that place a good deal

---

* *Salmo fontinalis.*

one way and another, and always the Diggers got me fish. The boys caught them. I did not trouble about them, for I had no rod, and have never cared much for bottom-fishing. And this was really bottom-fishing; for the boys would hunt for a certain white grub that lived in the roots of the reeds, and this they used as bait.

Now a bear, going nightly to some place of his affection, crossed the stream near the bottom of the valley at about the same point each time. So I had good hopes of intercepting him with a bullet, and went out one night with that intent. The August moon was full. And before I had gone very far I saw in an opening between the trees a bit of a tree-trunk, upon which I thought to sit and smoke my pipe and listen to the owls. But as I prepared to do this the trunk gave a grunt, and was not a trunk any more, but an old Digger Indian wrapped in his blanket and lying out full-length upon his back. I apologised and passed on.

I have mentioned this occurrence for nothing else in the world but to explain my introduction to the old Digger, whom I saw again next day. He had seen something of civilisation in the Yo Semite Valley, so we patched up a conversation fairly well.

I happened to have in my cap a trout-fly—one usually has; they rest there from season to season. I tried to explain that in England we caught trout with these. The Digger looked derision, and the more when I told him it would catch his trout all right. "No, no good. Only Indian," pointing to himself. "Well," I answered, "*I* will catch you one."

So borrowing a line (such a line !) from the boys, I cut down a willow bough, put on my fly with its five or six inches of gut collar, and, feeling that the honour of England hung upon me, got to work.

The only way, of course, in which anything could be done was by letting the line run out on the top of the water, so that the stream took it under the bushes, and then the fly could be worked a bit.

Of course the trout wouldn't look at that fly. It scared them. They fled from it. At first the Digger boys looked on. But they soon grew tired of watching a lunatic at work, and left. I will not trouble to give any details of the performance; they would not pass the columns of *The Field* in the very dullest season. But the one constant feature of the day was my old Digger. He never left. He shadowed me. Sitting always just behind and puffing at his pipe, he never spoke; he only watched and waited, only waited and watched. No Sphinx ever looked across the desert with more persistent, more eternal eyes. He grew to seem the very Genius of the place, muttering spells below his breath.

Well, I fished on till the evening, but it was ever the same story; fish were everywhere, but not a fish would come. One hates to confess oneself beaten, and the triumph of the old wizard of a Digger would have been bad to bear. But it really seemed a hopeless waste of time; and I had just determined to chuck it up, when behind a stone I saw the waving of a tail. How I sighed for my old "Farlow" and just two yards of fine-drawn gut! Well, I pulled myself together for a final try. A ridiculous idea had come into my head.

But I would not begin yet; for at that moment there was a sound of horse's hoofs, and riding down the valley came a loafer from the gold diggings; his long legs straddled down on either side of a rat-tailed screw. He pulled up to look. So I moved down a yard or two and feigned to be trying for a fish. Impatient for him to go, and not in the best of tempers, the cheer I gave him was not great. He watched for a few minutes and then rode off with the laconic summary, "Guess you want a finer pole."

But he was gone. Now for my *pis aller*—my forlorn hope.

Cholmondeley Pennell, in the delightful book that was my fishing oracle as a boy, remarks that the black chub fly may be improved by threading a bit of white kid on the bend of the hook. Perhaps the fish take it for a gentle. Well, this was my idea. If, I thought, I could only put on a bit of kid perhaps this fish would take it for the Digger boys' grub. But white kid-gloves were optional in that valley. I had not brought mine. So—it was the resource of despair—I snipped off a tiny piece of my pocket handkerchief, put that on, fell on my face, wormed my way to the edge, dropped the fly on the water, worked it down, down, till it was caught by the little current that played round the further side of the stone. Well, what possessed that fish I do not know and didn't care. But he took it! By Jove, he *took* it! It was ticklish work the getting him out, but after a minute or two of wading and grabbing and careful wiles, he was out on the grass and he was mine. He was not a big fish, but a fish he was. What cared I what his size might be Enough that the charm was broken, the wizard was beat.

Never a word said the old Digger, nothing beyond a grunt. Only he wrapped his blanket round him and strode away to join his squaws.

Fish the Second.

Through a garrison town on the south coast runs a little stream. Showing now, now running on beneath the streets, it empties at last into the harbour by a small sluice-gate. But above the town, away up among the chalk hills, it is a beautiful trout stream, though the fish do not run very large.

At one point of its progress is a big mill-pond. When the mill is not at work, the stream runs by other gates right beneath the miller's house. And here the water is deep—ten feet deep perhaps—but so clear that in the sunshine everything upon the bottom may be plainly seen. And two big fish were always lying here, one with a broad white scar upon his shoulder. Many had tried to take them, but without success. Apparently they never moved. I tried them myself with the worm; letting it gently down and watching till it hung in front of and even touched their noses. But only once did the white-scarred fish condescend to take the worm, and even then, before I could strike, it was shot out of his mouth to a distance of several inches, so great was the scorn of the fish.

An Irish regiment was quartered in the town just then, and belonging to it were three or four keen fishermen. Their luck with the fish was no better than my own.

About five o'clock one evening, at the Club, these anglers' conversation turned on the white-scarred fish. I suppose I had been going it a bit, for one of them presently came out with a "Look here, I'll lay five to one you don't catch him before we leave."

"Done," was my answer, "and I'll lay the same odds that I catch him within the next four-and-twenty hours." The bet was taken.

The regiment was going in a week's time; so that if I lost my money, I might still win it back before time was up.

I felt certain that both these were very old fish, who in all probability never moved at all in the daytime nor ever touched a fly, but went roving round at fall of night to feed on smaller fish.

Now it was impossible to work a minnow properly in this pool, especially at night, because the water was full of vernal water-starwort that everywhere stood up from the bottom in great solid pillars of emerald green.

But I had a small but heavy silver minnow—the name of the pattern I forget, but every one knows it. If you sink them rapidly they spin freely by their own weight. This I took and slipped off to the pond, which was three miles or so away.

The short remaining time of daylight was spent in studying as minutely as possible the geography of the weeds. Every little channel I tried to learn by heart, and every lump of weed all round the immediate spot. And then I sat on the wall and waited.

For there was a wall round the mill end of the pool, and from the foot of the wall a stoned escarpment followed down, curved to the water-edge. By the wall ran the cart-road, and across this was the miller's house, not seven yards from where I sat. I could see the miller's wife and daughter working at their sewing machines by the light of two paraffin lamps.

It was dark now—time for the deed to be done. Lightly the minnow was swung out over the wall and dropped upon the pool.

THREE FISH

Well, it was the work of a second. For *as the minnow touched the water* there was a rush, a tug, and a fish was on. It was too dark to make out much, though I could feel he was a biggish fish. But there was little or no fight in him, and he never travelled far. And it was not long before I could just see his belly turn up white.

He was safely on, but how to get him out! He was far out of reach, and to climb down that slippery wall in the dark, hampered by rod and landing-net, with any chance of success was clearly impossible.

I shouted, I yelled. But do you think those women could hear? Not a bit of it. What with their sewing machines and the rush of the water through the gate, my voice was lost.

But the high-road ran behind the mill, and so it fell that Policeman X, passing that way on his beat, heard loud cries and, suspecting murder, came to see.

I always remember that policeman with gratitude. He was indeed a friend in need. Tips? I don't believe it crossed his mind. He was a true sportsman, and could not see a good fish lost. He took in the situation at a glance. "You just wait a moment, sir," he said, "and *I'll* get 'im out."

He knocked at the door, he borrowed the two lamps, he placed them on the wall on either side, he took the landing-net, he clambered down somehow (a very nasty undertaking), he whipped up the fish, and returned safely. By lamplight, by a constable on duty—was ever a trout so landed before!

We weighed him in the mill. Three pounds and a half and rather more, with a white scar on his shoulder. I bore him off in triumph and tramped back to the Club.

My friends as I entered were busied in a game of pool. In the mouth of the fish I fixed a small coachman fly, broke off the trace and sent the fish in by the waiter on a dish; then I lay low to watch the tableaux through the peephole of the billiard-room. My rival's initial exclamations were not meant for publication. But I can hear now the supreme disgust with which he ended up his comments "and a *coachman* too!" As if it were adding insult to injury for such a menial to have done the trick.

Well, the fish was cooked forthwith, and we had him for supper with as much of "the boy" as the stakes would run to, and in the safety of after supper I confessed to the minnow.

Should any of those good fellows ever chance to

come across these lines I hope they will recall with as much pleasure as I that evening at the Club.

We duly toasted Policeman X.

Fish the Third.

Six grilse in two hours, and all in one long pool, — would be good work anywhere. But that was my record nevertheless one day on a tributary of the Tweed.

Only two were clean-run fish. The others were red fish that long had lain in the pools below waiting for a spate. For we had been suffering from weeks of drought. But at last the storm had burst upon us, and for days the river had been raging down as red and thick as coffee-grounds. The fish had run up madly; throwing themselves up over the caul in hundreds—a beautiful sight to see. But now the water had fined down nicely, the pools were quiet, and the fish were taking well.

I had begun fishing at three o'clock. At five or so I had landed my sixth grilse, and by half-past five was into a big fish.

He had been rising all the afternoon more or less, and very quietly, close to a willow bough off an island half-way across the stream. Forty yards above was the big salmon leap, and some sixty perhaps below, a smaller fall with a very nasty run of boulders and broken water.

A man who had been trying hard for this fish, without any luck, had gone up at five o'clock for tea. My chance had come. I gave the fish a good rest of nearly half an hour and then threw over him. It was a poor, moth-eaten looking fly—the body of claret with a twist of varnished tinsel, and a dirty speckled wing. But I chose it for two good reasons: it was the exact opposite of the fly my neighbour had been using, and, better still, it had often brought me luck.

At the very first cast I moved the fish, but he came short; at the second I saw nothing of him; at the third there was a swirl, he took it under water, turned and hooked himself.

A good deal has been written about the proper time to stike a salmon. It is all a waste of words. A salmon, of course, moves more deliberately than a trout, as becomes the heavier fish. Others have their own experience, mine is this. Nine times out of ten if you strike at a salmon you whip the fly out of his mouth. Nine times out of ten, if you leave him alone *and he means taking it*, he will hook himself. "An artist would have taken that tenth fish, and that is just where it comes in." Well, possibly. I am not an artist. Let us get back to our fish.

For some time I saw nothing of him. Keeping deep down, he headed up straight for the fall. Stop him? Not a bit of it, though I butted him all I knew. Bang into the white water he ran and lay still as a log beneath the foam. Indeed, he might have been a log for all the response I could obtain to my best efforts. I hung on and shouted for help.

This was the village pool. At the side of it was a big flour-mill employing a good many hands. Presently some one noticed the situation, and out came the miller with offers of help. Well, we exhausted all the usual devices, from jarring on the rod to throwing of stones. All to no purpose. Move he would not till it suited his lordly will. But at last he moved a little and began boring about, and then the pull on him told, and like a flash he was down the stream. Out ran the line like lightning till the reel shrieked again.

I could not follow him, because trees, growing on the edge of the pool, prevented me. He headed straight for the lower fall, and was now close upon it. Only a yard or two of line was left on the reel. Once over that fall, once among the rocks, and I might say goodbye to him for ever. It was a tug of war and chance it! But nothing gave and he was stopped. Right in the smooth water at the head of the fall he was stayed and then came working back, but up and down a bit, giving me a chance of reeling up. And then like a race-horse he started again, making hard for the upper fall. And as he came he flung himself clear of the water more than once—a glorious, silvery, clean-run fish.

Most of the village was there by that time, and the excitement was immense. Thirty pounds, five-and-thirty, at any weight they guessed him, but who ever guessed rightly yet?

He did not reach the upper fall: I brought him back instead. And then when opposite me he ploughed straight down and lay behind and beyond a stone—a biggish lump and very well known. You might make it out at low water.

From this position nothing would induce him to move, and every moment I expected the line to come back in my face, frayed through by the rock. But it held.

About ten minutes of this, and a thunderstorm came on which drove my supporters for shelter.

Fortunately it was short, but it was very sharp and left me wet to the skin. One by one the village again turned up with lots of advice, as is always the way, but no sensible action. Would no one wade in for me and move that fish? No one, of course. Indeed, by general consent there was only one person at all capable of tackling such a difficulty—a downright good fisherman and no mistake, and that was Mick, the mole-catcher. But Mick was away at his traps. Somebody thought he could fetch him.

It was seven o'clock, and Mick was long in coming. There was nothing for it but to hang on. I was staying at a house some five miles off, and that evening there was a rather particular dinner. Anyhow, I was wet and cold and wanted that fish out.

At last there was a shout and a crowding round that told of the coming of Mick. He was a long, foolish-looking chap, evidently flattered by his distinguished reception.

But Mick was not such a fool as he looked. Wade in there? Not he. Not for twenty salmon: he knew that pool too well. So there was nothing for it. I must go, and Mick should take the rod.

Hanging up on a tree was a huge landing-net with a good strong handle, not the sort of thing I should

E

care to leave by my salmon pool, but still with this they were wont, as they said, to land "the gentlemen's fish." Taking this I started in. "Whatever you do, keep the point of the rod up." This was my parting injunction to Mick, and Mick grinned a ready reply, for he was a great fisherman.

Well, it was horrid. The water was running very strong and deep, and even with the help of the landing-net handle I had much ado to keep my feet. I could only move sideways and move by inches with my face towards the stream. And even when the stone was reached, it was worse than ever. For it was a pretty ticklish thing standing without support, while with the landing-net an effort was made to stir the fish who lay so awkwardly beyond the stone.

It was done at last. For one instant the line flashed off like lightning, and then, singing past my face, came the loosened fly and—all was over.

Mick the mole-catcher had lost his head and *dropped the point of the rod!*

What they said to Mick I do not know. A village is rightly jealous for the good name of its heroes. The only word I caught was the parting slow remark of the old miller as he turned to go, " Ay, lad, but it was a braw fish."

I don't think I said much. It took some time for me to work my way back to the bank, and by the time I reached it rage had given place to settled sadness. There are times when words can help you, but there are times when words can not.

This was one.

MEMORIES

MEMORIES

Down the Brook.

A COUNTRYMAN shut up in the heart of a great city. Yes, an anomaly. But it has happened before, and will happen again.

What is left him? What but memory? Think for one moment of this subtle thing. Not a physiologist of them all can explain its methods or say even, "Here it lies." "White matter," "grey matter," "molecular changes"? Are they laughing at us? Where have they all been stored, these facts of years ago? Unsuspected, hidden away, keeping quiet, evading all detection, not to be apprehended by any conscious grasp. But there all the while—alive, potential, to start, perhaps years hence, into life, and challenge us once again with the problem of memory that laughs at time and space·: memory that is never really far away, but sometimes drives us, sometimes follows where we call; that may be commanded but may not be bound; man's master and man's servant, his blessing and his curse.

It is still August, and the days are intolerably hot. Not a breath moves in the pitiless, shelterless streets. Hot air, hot pavement, hotter dust that makes the infrequent water-cart a sound from heaven. Opposite my window there is a forge. I have scarcely noticed it before to-day. There it is, with its open doorway all red inside like a wizard's cave, with the hammers ringing on the anvil and the sparks showering out of the big flue. And sure enough—as if there were no heat outside—there are children crowding round the doorway—the little old-faced children I pass so often in the streets, but coloured and transfigured by the glow.

And now I notice that a mighty oak-tree hangs its branches over the forge. Something about this tree makes it seem strangely familiar. I fancy it must be that long black scar, curiously shaped and jagged, that shows where lightning has been at work. That indeed it is. I am standing opposite the forge of my childhood. It is four o'clock on a summer afternoon, and the children are coming down the hill from school.

The forge was thatched when first I knew it. The

sparrows used to drill this roof with holes, flying away with long straw streamers to their nests. "Thatcher Dick" was always patching and casing it, and it never had a whole new suit of thatch.

But after a time the place changed tenants. The new man had been a smith in Woolwich Arsenal. "Arsenic" was as near as the carters could get to it; and none of us knew where it was, and few of us what it meant. It was enough that he had made cannons for the soldiers. For on still days you might hear a heavy booming over the hills, which some said were "cannon-guns, they reckoned." Anyhow, we stood in awe of him as a very Vulcan, and were not surprised when the thatch was replaced by a beautiful roof of new red tiles, and a second fire and bellows placed inside.

There was a good trade going in those days before the dawn of cheap machinery. Old turn-rice ploughs lay about round the door waiting for their newly pointed shares. Big horses would stand with heads down, in a brown study, lifting at intervals a heavy foot for the trying-on of shoes; and everything told of regular and ready custom.

At the top of the hill beyond the forge rises the church spire—a beautiful, tapering shingle spire, as many are in Kent. On the walls inside the tower are the "charity boards," scored all over with those strings of chalked figures which express the art-language of the bell-ringers. Overhead is the thud of the constant pendulum, ponderous and slow.

The sexton was head over the ringers in those days. He was a long and lank old man, and this, I suppose, was why every one called him "Spider," for his real name was John. Many a time have I stood by him in the tower while he tolled out the bell. There was a varying scale of pulls, so that one might know whether a man, woman, or child had died. In each long interval Spider would settle himself upon a trestle, puff at his pipe, and become oracular on bobs and singles. He was always oracular —it was his style—as became the leading politician of the White Horse over the way. He was loyal to the Church as far as his lights went, and honoured her in her servants after his own fashion. "He had buried three parsons," Spider used to say, "and from what he could see of the gout and other ailments he reckoned he should live to bury four!"

Spider was mole-catcher to the parish generally, and a very clever one he was. Many a lesson we had as boys from him. He taught us not to set the traps in the open field, but in banks, and especially in gateways where the ground is hard. You must probe about until you hit off a "run," and then, should you find the inside smooth and round, you may be sure it is a main one and much frequented. In such a place as this, Spider, in February and March, when the moles were running, would sometimes take two dozen before he lifted his traps. He despised the new spring traps, preferring a wire noose and a hazel or ash "bender," which would fly up and swing the victim clean out of the ground, where it would hang like the fish outside the tackle-makers' shops, and soon the bushes all about would become filled with spitted moles.

I am afraid as boys we did not take very kindly to church. We were not allowed to walk in the puddles by the way, and there was a rigidity, generally, about Sunday that oppressed us. Sometimes, however, it was a bit better. When there were friends staying in the house we were turned loose into a big box-pew. This gave grand chances for the making of paper pellets. We usually confined ourselves to flipping these at marks inside the pew, but in moments of great daring we chose a more tempting target. The clerk sat immediately in front of the pew, and the round bald patch on the back of his head offered a mark few boys could long resist.

And then there were minor diversions. One Sunday in each year we knew as "Starling Sunday." It was a movable feast, but usually fell about Whitsuntide.

It was that first Sunday in the year on which the young starlings were to be heard chirruping under the eaves. Every few minutes the arrival of an old bird with a grub was hailed with a chorus of clamour. Sometimes a bat—"flittermice" the people call them—would wheel up and down and round and round till the eye was giddy with watching. And then a robin or a swallow would become imprisoned, and in early spring the hybernated tortoiseshell butterflies would flutter up and down the royal arms in the east window. Our most constant visitor was a little toad, who lived beneath the stone step of the side door. He used to come out when the stones got very hot, and sit winking a thin film over his red eyes, meditative and composed.

Every few years some of the shingles used to slip down from off the spire, and then "Steeple Jack" was sent for. He only asked a good stout rope, and there he would swing by the hour at a dizzy height like some big spider.

But "Steeple Jack" never mended the broken iron cross beneath the vane. It had lost a bit of floral work, which Peter Yeo, the gamekeeper, had knocked off as a lad with a shot from his crossbow.

Peter was our daily oracle: our *deus ex machinâ* in every strait. If a pike ran off with a trimmer, Peter fished it out; if the puppies were ill, Peter put them right; and though I must own to a feeling, come upon me since, that gunpowder and tobacco were but a limited pharmacopœia, still the greatest discoveries are ever the simplest, and nothing succeeds like success. He was privileged to keep a cow, which he had won as a calf one Boxing-day at the "Spar Shoot." For Peter, though an old man, had an eye as keen as a hawk's. They used to say that Peter young was a match for any five men about. "Knock one down, t'other come on," was how they used to put it. Be that as it may, he was a huge man of immensely powerful frame, and seemed to us boys a very Colossus of Rhodes as he stood in his favourite attitude as umpire at the village cricket-matches.

The real old Kentish dialect survived in Peter and in many of his day.

"Why, Peter, what ever has happened to old Chum?" we asked him one day, as the old dog came along bleeding from sundry scars about the muzzle.

"Well, sir, it was like o' this 'ere," said Peter. "I was a-coming past the farm geate, when all at onst I be bothered if that rusty-coout ship-dog didn't roosh out at my old Chum, and firedly massa*creed* him—sure*lie*!"

The natives, generally, showed a remarkable ingenuity in supplementing a limited vocabulary by words most aptly coined.

"No, sir," remonstrated the bailiff's wife with the curate, "my boy *he* wouldn't get into *no* trouble by hisself; 'tis the other chaps as *coyduckses him* away." The same woman excused herself for sending up bad eggs to the House on the plea that "the hens were getting so very old."

To return for one moment to Peter Yeo. We came back from school one summer day to find poor Peter ill in bed. He said it was only "the jandrers"; that he had netted us some new flams for ferreting, and would soon be about again. But his face was as yellow as a guinea, and the next day but one he died. Peace to thy shade, dear Peter; I shall never know a truer or a kindlier friend.

Just below the forge a little brook runs under the road. One field higher up it is scarcely to be distinguished from the bog, which earlier in the year is one golden wealth of marsh-marigold. The bog water is quite red, for there is iron in the soil. Long ere the days of Sub-wealden exploration the ore was worked, and such local names as "Furnace House," "Iron Mill," point back to foundries that long have ceased to be. The king was wont to get his cannon from these foundries, and there is a quaint old field-piece on the rectory lawn which was found when the dam of the big pond broke one year, and all that summer the pond lay dry.

But here the brook goes tinkling on about the roots of alder-bushes whose leaves meet overhead. The redpoles love these alders when they come in later summer, and twitter there in little parties all day long, hanging back-downwards, and pecking into the old seed capsules for what little they may find. Between the alders the stream is spanned by bramble and dewberry and boughs of guelder rose, and roofed so close that only by the most curious peering may one see the chequered sunlight playing on the stones. There! that was a trout. You will not see him again—he has flashed himself into a rat's hole after the manner of his kind. Very different are the ways of these little troutlets from those of the full-fed aristocrats of the larger streams. Both are *salmo fario*, but this is one whose tale of doubtful dinners gained on worms and caddises is plainly told by his eel-like body and his head like a miller's-thumb; and the other is—what this would be, could they change places for a year or so. Many a long day of the summer holidays would we boys spend in the taking of these trout. Sometimes we tickled them; but when the pool was too deep for this we, with great labour of childish arms, would throw a dam across the pool's head and bale the water out; and so, catching the fish, transfer them to the big pond above. When, lo, a wonder! A year or two gone by, and we would retake them with fly or minnow, noble trout of two and three pounds weight. The trout were our noblest quarry, but the brook held, besides these, some store of fry, stone-loach and miller's-thumbs. The kingfishers, too, from their favourite perch on the dead roots of a fallen alder, used to catch the minnows, and even sticklebacks in spite of their spines.

Here the brook widens to a little shallow, where the cattle come to drink. In one of the hollows which their feet have trod an unwonted splashing is going on. A pike, scarce three inches long, has caught a minnow. Small as he is, there is the same cruel look in his ugly little head, and the same ferocity in his attack as if he were a twenty-pounder. He has caught the minnow by the middle, and jerks him from side to side as a robin jerks an earthworm on the lawn. A larger pike would have no need to shake his prey; he would seize it in the same fashion and, retiring to his hole, bolt it head foremost, as every angler knows.

Below the shallow is a flight of little terraces formed of sandstone flags that marks the position of a worn-out water-gate; and then the river and the weir.

The farmers say that, what with the river choking up and summer floods, they have no need of water on the land. Be this as it may, the gates are gone, and only the posts and terraces are left. The water, by its constant working between the stones, has hollowed out quarters for a family of water-shrews. By peeping motionless between the stems of an alderbush we may see them at their play. As they chase one another about the pools they look like streaks of silver light from the bubbles entangled in their fur. Round they go, and in and out, in the mazes of the water-shrew quadrille; now out of sight beneath the flags, and now popping up in the most unlooked-for corner. Every now and then one will land upon the stones, and, giving himself a single shake, sit there for a moment basking in the sun, not wet one whit, but with a coat as soft and dry and shining as a mole's.

By the River.

It is the sun that shows us Nature's face to-day, and tells the story of her children's lives. It is the sun which sped the tiny feet upon the hill, and joyed them so they could not choose but play. It is the sun that set the shrew-mice dancing in the pools. It is the sun that is filling all the air with a sense of music—the sound of myriad insects that you cannot see. It is the sun that draws the big pike from the depths, and leaves him lying atop of the weeds, as still and ugly as a crocodile on banks of Nile.

It is the sun that, laying a broad hand upon the stream, smoothes all his eddies out and sends him on between his banks of glistening goss, not babbling loud as is his wont, but murmuring softly in his sleep.

Yes, the river is very sleepy to-day. Truth to tell, however, it never really hurries save at flood. It lacks the boulders and the rapids of the North and West. A dipper flying here from mountain burns would lose all joy of life in the slow reaches of this southern stream.

Yet the sleepy river has its share of living interests, not few and not unvaried, and all especial to quiet valleys such as this.

There, resting on the end of a bough of half-sunk willow, is a moorhen's nest. The water-rats use it as a dinner-table now, for the dusky babies tumbled out of it and into the water full six weeks ago.

No water-rat makes those circles that come from under the willow stub. They are too wide and heavy. No; it is the water-hen herself. She dives with a quiet splash, and a chain of tell-tale bubbles marks her way to the opposite bank. There is little shelter on the further side, so she will not scramble out till we are gone. But, keeping still and looking closely, the surface of the stream is broken ever so gently by one tiny wavelet that circles round some red thing like a winter hip, that was not there before. It is the scarlet patch upon the moorhen's head. This is all that we can see, close as we may look. But bright and keen are the eyes that watch us, and will watch until we go. And then if, ere the distance grows too great, we just glance back across our shoulder, we shall see the bird creep upwards from the water, threading deftly the thin low sedges, with white and flirting tail. A beautiful bird is the water-hen, and well-beloved of fishers and such as move by streams.

More life can be seen in an hour by the river than a whole long day upon the hills. Look up, and you will notice that birds that fly inland high overhead follow the river as a blind man feels a clue.

Above the broad flat meadows the peewits are twisting in eccentric circles, crying all the while, for their first eggs were crushed by the roller and the dredge, and their second broods are not long hatched. They always run some dozen yards or so before they rise, and will not light beside their young lest these should be discovered, and so they tumble and twist above our heads with sounding wings, and "peewit!" without pause, and so reproachfully that innocence, with no designs on eggs or young, feels shame to have approached so dear a spot.

A little black-pated bird whips out from under the bank and flits ahead. He perches on a bit of waving rush, raising his top-knot, and seeming to defy the world; but as we approach he flies off, to settle again some few yards further on. He will do this a dozen times or more. The bird is the reed-bunting, and this is his own little manœuvre for the safety of his nest.

Do you see that little grey-brown, bright-eyed bird, slipping mouse-like about the sloes? It is the sedge-warbler. It seems almost incredible that from so small a throat could come such a torrent of sound! Yet so it is. For a song which, without being strictly music, is indeed a joyful noise, commend me to the sedge-bird. All day long he sings, and often far into the night, and though he should have settled into sleep a sudden noise will wake him into song again.

Be silent now, for we are nearing sacred ground. Here the stream divides, to join again at a point a little higher up. But, so circling, it closes in a fair round island, known this many a day as "The Swan's Nest"—a good name, for it lies indeed like some big nest, deep down here in the heart of this unfrequented valley; and all around stretch the broad water-meadows, where the black, long-horned cattle fare so well. On the first slopes of the rising ground beyond is many a furrowed garden, frothed by the yellow spray of hops that top the poles; and then wave on wave of purple heather rolls on and on, to break at last and lose itself among the sheep-fed hollows of the thyme-scented Surrey hills.

The backwater itself is jewelled about with flowers of every hue—tall spikes of purple and yellow loose-strife, whole beds of blue forget-me-not, and that other violet-blue of meadow cranes-bill, with purple comfrey and giant water-dock.

On the other side flows the stream itself in pool and shallow, by steep banks where the gnarled roots of the pollard oak-trees make a hiding for the otters. Wide they stretch their arms across the island and wide across the stream, and underneath them lie the big chub, taking with sounding lips the drowning moths. Chub-fishing is not reckoned for much as sport; and yet, to throw a fly without fouling among those boughs, and so deftly that it shall drop lightly as an insect from the leaves, is no mean test of skill. And many a practised hand on Test or Itchen owes all its prowess to 'prentice-days in this so small a school.

There upon the shallow stands a heron waiting till an eel shall move in the mud. Gaunt and still he stands—a grim magician brooding some new spell.

But now a single bubble rising is followed by a tiny cloud of mud. Slight as is the symptom, it is all the watcher needs. A half-step, a lightning stroke, and that sharp beak has transfixed an eel. But even then, the bird, warned by some unwonted sight or sound, rises into the air on slow and labouring wing, the eel writhing in fruitless efforts to escape.

Behind the island stands an old man telling sheep. He wears the smockfrock and moleskin breeches of his day. It is old John Roffey, the hero of many a ploughing-match in earlier years. A bit too stiff to manage ploughing now, he looks as hard and hale as an old oak.

"I was a-wondering whatever that 'ere bird had got in his mouth," says the old man; "I could see as there was somethin' a-twizzlin'."

"Why, John, what good eyes you have got! That is because they are blue eyes. They are always the best. All the best rifle-shots have blue eyes."

"My wife's brother's son," returns the old man, losing the point, "is a hem-an-all fine shot with a rifle, they tell me. Lives down at Hadlow," jerking his thumb over his shoulder.

"Ah, I suppose he is in the volunteers?"

"No," says John very deliberately, "no, I doan't know as he was ever anything-*in*. But, there," he adds sententiously, "he must have been something some*when* or he couldn't never have been nothin'."

There are truisms which defeat us by a sense of hopelessness. I suppose it was just the appeal from this state of paralysis which herewith shook me from my reverie. But even as I woke memory wove itself into a rhyming measure, and thus it ran:

THE SWAN'S NEST.

I knew in the days that are long ago,
   In the land that I love the best,
Of a cradled spot in a slumberous vale
   Called ever " The Old Swan's Nest."

And never an island lay more dear
   In the purple of Indian seas ;
For all that it was but a tangle-space
   And a score of pollard trees.

MEMORIES

Old oaks whose arms at set of sun
   Wove pictures weird and black,
Whose roots crept feeling round the sides
   Like the folds of a python's back.

For the sand was fretted and hollowed about
   By the stream's unresting play;
Except where the eddies, gone tired to sleep,
   In silence and shallow lay.

And here like lamps the lilies shone,
   And king-cups gemmed the spot,
All fringed to the side with the ruby bell,
   And the turkis forget-me-not.

And here the crowfoot bloomed, who folds
   Her beauty from the moon,
And feathered milfoil here that holds
   The dew until the noon.

Low-circling have I often seen,
   About the fall of night,
The white owl hunt the mouse, so soft
   You might not hear her flight.

And then the blue wood-dove would come
    To rest; and squirrels bring
The last nut in; and with the dark
    The black mole-cricket sing.

An old grey fox had his kennel there;
    And never a hound so fast,
But he led him the best of a ten-mile point,
    To beat him by craft at last.

When his bark rang out in the moonlit night,
    Away on the open moor,
The sheep-dog moved in his sleep and growled
    At his post by the hen-house door.

He would seize the feeding water-fowl
    By creeping in the sedge,
When the moon was hid by a long black cloud
    With a silver-crested edge.

I have met the dawn as it touched the stream,
    And whitened the dew in the dell,
But the dove was abroad in the beanfield then,
    And a heron stood sentinel.

And hares were running rivalries
    About the island grass,
And lazy kine would hardly rise
    And let the angler pass.

It lay in a nameless peace alway,
    As a deep enchanted dale
Lies under a spell, at a wizard's will,
    In some old fairy tale.

But this no fairy wand had touched,
    No wizard charm was there,
But only Nature's, at the will
    Of Him who crowned her fair.

And He unseen, as seen of yore,
    Walks still the thronging street,
But here it seems there comes more clear
    The echo of His feet.

Where never woodman swung the axe,
    Nor ploughshare turned the sod,
But Nature smiles as Eden smiled
    New from the touch of God.

And when the shadows deepen down,
    And light dies in the west,
Were it mine to tell ere the passing-bell
    Where I should lie at rest:—

Not where the city's agony
    Goes up the city's prayer ;—
Not in the Minster's reverent pride,
    For all the heroes there ;—

But when the shadows deepen down,
    And evening calls to rest,
I could choose to lie beneath His eye
    In the peace of "The Old Swan's Nest.'

A CHILD OF THE PEOPLE

A CHILD OF THE PEOPLE

WHERE lies the charm of running water? In the play of light and movement certainly, but chiefly, I think, in sound. The loveliest, sweetest sound in all Nature is the tinkling of a little stream. Only two musical instruments besides can give you this. One there is—and you must guess it; and another— and that other the throat of the starling. It is at sunrise and at sunset that the starling chiefly sings. Even on the chimney-pots of grimy, grim old London he will sit and sing for all you cannot hear him. Only you know by his ruffled feathers and tremulous wings that he is singing the song of the rippling water.

And in London, too, the water sings its song.

Under the iron streets the water comes, and through miles of leaden pipes and hidden windings, but always saying over to itself, it cannot so forget it, the music taught it of the streams, till at last it plashes in the marble basin with its message of love for the hurrying crowd. "Stay," it says, "stay with me. Why do you pass so fast and heedless, with downcast eye and troubled, careworn brow? What is gold but a mocking phantom, and the seeking it but sorrow and death in life? Look up, up between the housetops; look away from the ugly, breathless pavement, to where the sun is shining and the sky is blue. I have something to tell you about that; I have things to say of beauty and purity and love. Stay and listen. Stay—" But no one stays; or only the children stay—yes, the children stay.

Under the walls of St. Paul's Cathedral is a drinking-fountain of some pretensions. It is all of marble and is fair and round. It is in that corner where the pigeons are. They are so tame, you know, that they will settle on your shoulders when you bring them bread to eat. I know a curious person from the country who keeps a little grain or bread-crumbs in his pockets, and feeds the pigeons that he meets with in his rounds. And one day it chanced that, after he had fed these the Pauline pensioners, he fell to leaning against the rim of the marble basin, and musing as he leant. Something, I suppose, in sight or sound awoke a note of pleasant memory that grew reflected in his face. For presently a voice said beseechingly beneath his elbow: "Let me see too." And looking down he was aware of the piteous figure of a hump-backed child. "Let me see too," repeated the little crooked thing, holding out its hands to help its prayer.

What a face it had! Such a thin, wan face, with a nameless expression that was not pain but told of it. A history of pain—of pain that began long, long ago, in father, in grandfather, in generations back perhaps. Of hunger, of cruelty, of—but it is a stale and well-worn story—you may read it by the drinking-fountains any day, and I be saved the telling.

Its name, it said, was Pete. Not a pretty name, but still, that was it—Pete. "Let me see too," said little Pete.

The curious person lifted little Pete, and raised him to the fountain's rim. Pete, it seemed, had expected to see something new and bright and strange. And so at first he showed a little disappointed, but only just at first. Then the fancy of the child was caught by the limpid jet, and it clapped its thin small hands and held them in the tinkling water, while such a smile lit up its face! So that the curious person longed to say: "Come with me, little' Pete, and I will take you to the music's home. I will show you such a pretty purling streamlet. I know it well. Out of the quiet hill it comes, and down the cradled valley passes, over beds of golden pebble, and into the clearest of crystal pools. In these the silver fish are glinting, and blue forget-me-nots grow round about, and high overhead meet the pink wild roses in arch and tangle and woven growths. And the stream like a glistening skein of silk goes on and on, till it comes to the ford below the cottage, and there the children play. And as it goes it sings a little song, and this is the burden of it. Only the song is far, far prettier than this, which is only its prose and sense:

> *See! I was born of a silver cloud*
> *That moves about the morning star;*
> *And I go singing soft or loud*
> *Where any children are.*
>
> *Mine is the touch of the dewy grass;*
> *The golden sunrise sent me here*
> *To greet the children as they pass,*
> *And tell them love is near.*

> *Mine is the peace of the quiet hill.*
> *I left the forehead of the day,*
> *When all the storms of night were still,*
> *To kiss a child at play.*
>
> *Mine is the gift of the power to live,*
> *Of the well of life—all-clear, all-true—*
> *And life, and all that life can give, .*
> *Dear child, is given to you.*

Something of this the curious person would have said, could little Pete have stayed to hear it. But it was scarcely half a minute before he was suddenly seized and carried away from the fountain and out through the iron gates with words of cursing that were worse than blows. A woman carried him so.

In the cathedral the organ is pealing, for the afternoon service is half-way through. It is the solo of the anthem. Listen: "—shall lead them unto living fountains of waters." Ah! there is something for little Pete. Think of that, little Pete —"*living* fountains." Just the ford to cross, and the other side to reach, and there the children play.

Happy as you were that moment by the fountain, as happy always. Oh, but happier far. For only where the living fountains are is life completely happy, for only there is life itself complete.

CANVEY ISLAND

CANVEY ISLAND

CANVEY ISLAND is only thirty miles from London, yet the two places are but little acquaint. Most Canvey Islanders have never been to London, and most Londoners have never heard of Canvey—unless, indeed, in connection with the problem of the disposal of London sewage. Yet its history may interest the curious, and the island itself will well repay a visit, for it is a quaint, old-world sort of place, and oddly un-English in many ways. It lies down the Thames, between Gravesend and Shoebury on the Essex shore. It is about five by three miles in extent, is as flat, and for the most part as treeless, as the Haarlem Lake, and like it has Dutch traditions, and is beloved of the Dutchman of to-day. Not that Canvey ever belonged to the Dutch; their connection with it came about in this way.

The Romans who embanked the Medway and the Thames doubtless did the same for Canvey, for they overran all the land about, and evidence of their industry may be found in the broken pottery which was often, until lately, washed up upon Leigh Beck, its extremest point. The Saxons have left ample evidence of their existence in local nomenclature, and the Danes of theirs in ruins which may still be traced; for here, under their leader Hasting, they were beaten in a great battle by Alfred, who took from them their fortress "Beamfleet"—*i.e.* Benfleet—on the mainland, "with deep and wide trenches," as Camden says. But the mighty engineers were gone, and things in Canvey went from bad to worse; until, in Camden's time, the tides had so far worked their will that all the arable land, of which there had been much, was ruined, for the island, he says, "is oftentimes quite overflowne, all save hillocks cast up, upon which the sheep have a place of refuge. For it keepeth about four hundred sheep." In 1621 (about eight years after Camden wrote) a principal owner, Sir Henry Appleton, with others interested in the soil, agreed, as appears by the records, to hand over one-third of the lands to one Joas Crappenburgh, a Dutch engineer, on condition that he should "in" and embank the island, ensuring it against future inroads of the sea. The land so made over is still called "Third-acre land." Crappenburgh's work was followed by a considerable immigration of Dutch, who sustained severe loss at the hands of their own countrymen during the Dutch incursions in the year of the Plague, and most of them then left. But if a pure Dutch name would be hard and a pure Dutch pedigree impossible to find, the round face, the heavy, square figure, and the stolid temper are characteristic of the Canvey Islander of to-day. As Lindisfarne, in short, is essentially Scandinavian, so Canvey is essentially Dutch.

Crappenburgh did his work conscientiously enough; but exceptional storms and spring-tides upset his calculations, and in 1735 so great was the damage to live stock from these causes (Canvey then fed near four thousand sheep) that the Third-acre land was by Act of Parliament saddled with a first charge—limited to 10*s.* an acre—towards the expenses of the wall; the remaining two-thirds were only to be rateable should more money be wanted—at that time a remote contingency. But the storms of 1881 wrought such frightful havoc that this land was charged as high as £1 per acre, a sum equal to the value of its rental.

The wall is finished now, and a solid bit of work it is; but the area it encloses is sadly contracted, and acres away over its eastern limit one may trace the old Dutchman's handiwork running down to the point, and see even now the remains of old fleets and ditches when the tide goes down. The point itself, indeed, has entirely gone to sea to the extent of half a mile within the last few years.

"The Lobster Smack," some time "The Sluice," Canvey's principal inn (she has, by the way, only two), lies just under the wall by Hole Haven, a little creek where barges and bawley-boats can ride. It is pleasant to lie in bed and watch the lights as the great steamers feel their way down Thames. Here, too, are rare chances for studying Dutch character, for the light that shines from the windows of the inn is a spell few Dutchmen can resist. And as the small Scheldt trading-boats come up the Thames, one by one they lay-to in the creek till morning light. London and Amsterdam have done many a stroke of business in a quiet way at this retired and convenient half-way house, for a bargain is wonderfully helped by a glass or two of old schiedam. This house has seen some curious doings in its time, before the white coastguard station put in an appearance, with its trim flower-beds, its flagstaff, and its handful of steady men. Mine host has often reason to be glad of the society of these useful allies when emergencies arise. For your Dutchman, stolid and phlegmatic in his sober moments, genial and somewhat noisy later on, has a tendency by ten o'clock or so to become wildly unmanageable and to run amuck at everything and everybody when closing time begins. Fortunately for himself the landlord is a strong and a plucky man, and is moreover ably seconded by his better half. There is an old flight-shooter, too, who can always be relied on in a row. Like most of those about the "Lobster Smack," he is honourably scarred. The loss of two fingers is the form it takes with him. Ask him how it happened, and he will say, "Well, sir, you see it was just like this 'ere. We was a-heftin' out a Dutchman one night, and I went for to hit his head, and he dropped sudden, and blest if I didn't drive right at that there beam."

Canvey contains about three thousand acres of land in all, and this was divided among eight different parishes, and was titheable to them. Whether the clergy of any of these parishes ever collected their tithes in person on this island I cannot say; but it is certain that for centuries no other consideration ever brought them there—the Church left the islanders absolutely alone. For marriage they had to trudge to their respective parish churches on the mainland, often a weary way; for burial they took their dead to Benfleet. A little chapel put up by the Dutch colonists in the seventeenth century was the first place of worship on the island. But the Dutch left, and the chapel fell into decay. It was rebuilt by one who held a small farm there, which he charged with £8 for a few sermons. This was slowly improved upon, and in 1715 a wooden chapel was consecrated by Compton, Bishop of London, "for 20 sermons a year." After a long interval some of the neighbouring clergy provided by contributions for a few more sermons, which were supplied in fine weather by the chaplain for the time being. Things have gradually improved, and for some years now Canvey has been happy in the possession of a vicar, a wooden vicarage, and a wooden church; while more recently, by a crowning and an almost superhuman effort, the island has been semi-parochialised. All the houses in Canvey are of wood, any heavier material is considered liable to disappear beneath the soft alluvial soil.

The cause of law and order was further promoted

a few years ago by the introduction of a policeman to the island for the first time. It would be impossible for those who have become familiar with "the bobby" to conceive the storm of scorn and indignation aroused by the arrival of this humble guardian of the peace. "*Canvey* don't want no p'lice," insisted a parlour orator; "let 'em keep to the mainland, *I* says. Ain't we already got the Clesiasticals?" The Ecclesiastical Commissioners having been compelled by bad times to take some land in hand themselves at the other end of the island, were regarded by the islanders as in some dim way an expression of authority and interference, and as the authors of all their woes. An abstraction known as "Guv'nment" has the same significance in the minds of rustics in other parts. "Fust chance I has," interposed our friend the flight-shooter, "I leads him down in the evening to the marshes beyent the fleets and takes the planks up"—a Christian determination which was much applauded. The fleets are deep and wide ditches which bisect the flats in all directions; they are crossed by narrow planks at rare intervals, and a stranger left down there on a cold winter's night would fare badly indeed.

Indiscriminate shooting has been the ruin of the

winter sport which once made Canvey so attractive to the wildfowler. But a visit to it in summer-time will well repay the lover of Nature. The bearded tit has long been driven away, and the prowling plant-stealer has hunted there unchecked, but what remains of flora and of bird-life is singularly characteristic and interesting. The trees of the island are mostly disposed in one small group, but this can boast a rookery.

One word as to the name "Canvey." Camden talks of "the island Convennos, which is also called Κώουννος," which, he says, Ptolemy mentions in his Geography. This name, he adds, is still retained in "Canvey." Had Ptolemy seen the island from a balloon, his use of the term would have been more intelligible, for the general shape of the island as then seen would be that of a pear; but given to a place as flat as a pancake it is an obvious misnomer. Further, the Canvey Islander would not have been careful to have preserved Ptolemy's word had they ever even heard of it. It has been suggested that Canvey, which often appears in records as "Canwe," "may *possibly* be a British name, since 'Canwe' in Welsh means bright, shining, glistening," and that this would fitly describe the appearance of the place, partly from the vast bank of shells on its eastern point, and more so from the fleet by which it was bisected as late as the time of Elizabeth. There are difficulties in the way of this derivation; but we will leave it as it stands, for want of a better.

IN THE LAND OF THE GREAT SPIRIT

IN THE LAND OF THE GREAT SPIRIT

Moving Up.

In the vernacular of the settlers, it is "Manitoba," but this is surely wrong. For it was named of the Indians away down the ages, centuries perhaps before the settler put foot in the land. To the Indian, with his small ambitions, his little needs, it was a perfect world. All that he could want lay there ready to his hand. The birch-tree gave him bark for canoes and drinking vessels, the pine-tree its roots for sewing-thread and string. Everywhere were fish, deer, buffalo, hare and grouse for food. From the moose he got skin for clothes and moccasins, and the sinew with which the squaws might sew them into shape.

It was too the land of mighty influences—the limitless prairie, the dark-hollowed forest, the lake to him like an inland sea. On the waters of the Assiniboine his canoe was tossed like a gopher-nut. Never so fiercely beat the sun upon the forest but suddenly it was Fall with poplar yellow and maple red; and then on the land fell the grip of winter and bound it in iron from farther south than he could wander to the ice-fields of the Hudson's Bay. From all this then there was no appeal. The Indian knew it. He confessed it in the name he gave his home—Manitou Ba, the Land of the Great Spirit.

It was in autumn, late September. I had come up from California to hunt moose. A seven days' journey or so brings one from San Francisco to Winnipeg. And about Winnipeg itself lie stretched the great prairies where the bison used to roam. There are at least two points about these prairies worth noticing—viz., the slews and the trails.

These slews are curious. They are about as wide as the dykes in Holland, and often run for a considerable distance quite as straight. And yet they are of course absolutely inartificial. They originate, it would seem, in springs, and then, as the action of the water wears away for itself a bed, they become in time the drains of the prairie. When they are damp or filled with water they are often of great service as obstacles which a prairie fire cannot pass. But when they are dry, they sometimes act in an exactly opposite manner. For they may form channels up which the fire creeps and spreads, often most insidiously, from place to place.

The trails are simply tracks formed on the grass by the passage of the Red River carts, or the horses of the old buffalo-hunters from point to point.

Even at night you can distinguish the trail from the surrounding prairie, for the trail shows up white in the darkness. And in the daylight you see why this is. The trails are covered with buffalo grass.* It is an oat grass. But whether it is the same as our own † I do not know.

Sometimes, although all the trail may be thick with buffalo grass, you will not be able to find any of the same kind in the prairie round about. Horses and cattle are very fond of this grass, and perhaps therefore we may explain its presence by supposing that it is by means of horses and cattle that the seeds become conveyed along the trails. But useful as the oat grass is as a guide at night, it often proves a delusive one. Not seldom the track takes you right up to the side of a quite impassable slew, and away on

* *Stipa spartea.* † *Avena pratensis.*

the other side you may see the oat grass stretching on as if to mock your helplessness. These trails are very, very old, and some of them can only be used, if at all, in the driest time. The fact is that not only is the bed of the slew constantly changing in depth owing to silting and deposit of vegetable growths, but that in this alluvial prairie soil the actual position and direction of the slews tend to alter. And the points of passage correspondingly change until in time the original crossing-place is quite forsaken. But still the oat grass goes on growing, a trap for the unwary in the years to come.

This, then, is the prairie where the boys ride on the beasts. The "rolling" prairie is mostly a misleading term, excepting in so far as it expresses the effect of waving summer grasses. It is only about the foot-hills that the prairie "rolls." Chiefly it is a flat of incalculable area where nothing but distance defeats the eye. In late autumn its colouring is monotonous and sombre, but in spring and summer it is ablaze with flowers from end to end. The flowers of the prairie are strikingly beautiful, varying greatly of course from place to place with altitude, latitude, and conditions of soil. A lovely and sweet-scented rose* that grows about six inches high; the purple aster; the Philadelphian lily that colours acre after acre in orange-red; anemones of many kinds; purple pentstemon—these are a few of the plants that flourish in the open. A low scrub and bush grows here and there in patches; and just as here in our own New Forest we read the different growths as a book because they show the nature of the ground, so there one learns very quickly the different kinds of scrub and what each can tell us as we go to hunt. The low-bush cranberries† and tamarac warn us of peat bogs; the wild strawberry tells that the forest is near; the silver berry bush‡ is a sure find for prairie chicken; the buffalo berry§ and the wild raspberry are beloved by the bear.

Wherever there is a large tract of land lying at a level the springs and drainage go to form a shallow lake. Not far from Winnipeg there is such a lake, some fifteen miles long, perhaps, by ten miles across, and of this I have something to say.

* *R. blanda.*
† *Vaccinium oxycoccus and V. macrocarpon.*
‡ *Elægnus argentea.*
§ *Shepherdia argentea.*

Travellers are expected to tell tales of hair-breadth escapes and exciting adventures. Now, although every man who has pushed far by himself in a wild country must have had some experiences of this kind, he will, if he is wise, keep them to himself. Only those who have been themselves in the same circumstances can appreciate them fairly; and for those who stay at home, or whose travels are confined to the well-beaten tracks of the Continent, they are only travellers' tales.

But almost every day some little thing comes about of which, as it ends well, little is thought, but which very easily might have been worse. Here is one that just goes to show how easy it is to be caught.

Touch and Go.

The horns of the moose were still in the velvet. So we dawdled along over the prairie, shooting prairie chicken, and the mallard and blue-winged teal that rose out of the slews. It chanced, then, that we went into camp by the side of the lake of which I have spoken, a famous lake for ducks. Out in the lake was an island where the pelicans bred.

Our tents were pitched on an open spot where

IN THE LAND OF THE GREAT SPIRIT

the dry grassy plain ran out in a little point right to the water's edge. But right and left of this there lay immense beds of reeds. They enclosed the lake on almost every side, and were in places something like two miles through. These reeds from top to water-line were about the height of a man's head.

The water, only a few inches in depth at the outside, grew deeper in the direction of the middle of the lake; but so gradually that a man might wade for perhaps a mile before the water reached his waist. Enclosed in the reed beds were numerous creeks and stretches of open water, too deep for any growth of reeds.

To wander then in these reed beds was to wander in a water-forest that completely shut out land or sky on any side. Around you reeds and water— the reeds far higher than your head. Directly above you your only bit of sky.

These reeds were the haunt of innumerable waterfowl, and into these reeds I went one evening to shoot. At first I skirted the edge of the reed beds. There were many things of interest all about. The American bittern skulked there almost until trodden upon. Beetles, allied to our Dytiscus, flying

122 IN THE LAND OF THE GREAT SPIRIT

by and dropping into the water, would rise again presently and fly off.

The quaint antics of the musk rats interested me very much. This creature is common in the marshy grounds of Manitoba. In general appearance it is like a miniature beaver, excepting that its tail is flattened from side to side and not from above downwards. When the lakes are frozen it still manages to keep its breathing holes open, by stuffing them with mud or moss. But it has the most extraordinary power of remaining for a long time under water. And I have more than once seen a startled musk rat come up under the clear ice, and remaining there for a few seconds dive down again. Under these circumstances it is supposed to exhaust the air in the lungs, breathing it in again as soon as it has been "converted by the oxygen in the water." But surely a sufficient explanation is this simpler one, that under the ice are many air bubbles to which the beast's instinct directs it. This animal builds from the bottom a large structure of reeds in the top of which, clear of the water, is its nest. There are no galleries, but only an entrance and a pophole.

But we wanted ducks for the pot, so presently, just

stopping to notice that the camp was on my left hand, I struck into the reeds. As I went on I broke off and bent down a reed here and there, as a clue for the journey back. Having shot as many ducks as I wanted, I turned to go home, for a flush across the sky told of sunset. At that moment I heard some way off what I believed to be the call of the summer-duck.* I was very anxious to get this bird for my collection, so I crept off in the direction of the sound. But sound travels a long way over water on a still evening, and it was some time before, having waded in water that was gradually getting deeper, a beautiful drake rose in front. I fired, and the bird fell. But though it lay still for a moment, it only had a broken wing, and presently it dived. And now I did a very foolish thing. Anxious to have the bird undamaged for mounting, and thinking that in that shallow water I could sooner or later run it down, I started in pursuit.

A stern chase is a long chase, especially after a crippled duck. He would dive ten yards or so, and I could trace him fairly well. Sometimes I was so close I almost grabbed him, but not quite, and then he would gain on me, reappearing disappointingly some

* *Aix sponsa.*

way ahead. Presently he took right up one of the open creeks. I followed. The water was about up to my waist. Up the length of the creek we went, but the water was all in his favour now, and I could move but slowly. There was no help for it. The next time he showed he was stopped by a shot and picked up. And then I turned to go home. But by this time it had grown sensibly darker, and with the change of light the whole aspect of the place had changed. Closely as I might look, I could not hit off the point at which I had entered the creek. At last finding something that looked like the opening, I struck into it. But it was a delusion. There was no track at all. In the excitement of the chase I had completely lost my bearings. I had no compass, and began to have doubts as to the direction of the camp. I had another good try to find the trail, and then stood still to think. My reflections did not help me much. For there was no doubt about it, I was lost.

All the red light had died out of the sky, and the stars were coming out. It was cold work in the water, and I did not like it much. I was pretty hungry too, and when you are hungry you feel the cold the more. I wandered about there in that reed forest for

IN THE LAND OF THE GREAT SPIRIT 125

some hours longer, never certain where I was going, whether towards the lake or from it (for the water deepened or got shallower so very gradually) until I really was about beat. Suddenly something caught my foot, and stumbling forward, I fell full-length right on to the top of a mound. This mound was a musk rat's house. Up this musk rat's house I dragged myself and presently stood on the top. And then I could see. There was the lake and there was the camp fire twinkling, but very far away. Over the camp but high up in the sky above it a big quiet star was hanging. Slipping very warily and slowly from my perch, I found that I could just manage to keep that star in view above the reeds. And so I followed it. Sometimes from looking at it so long and anxiously it seemed to change, and then I even wondered if it were the same. Sometimes for a moment I lost it altogether. It was one of the worst walks I ever took. But perseverance won at last. Beneath my feet was the solid prairie with the camp not very far away. It was about an hour after midnight when I tumbled into the tent.

This was the more remarkable because as a rule the musk rats do not build very far from the bank. But either the lake had been much lower in the summer, or the nest was really near some small island which in the darkness I could not see.

But soon it was time to be moving on if we were to be ready for the moose. And as we shall now be alone with the Indians, it may be worth while to say a little about them. The following, as a general impression, will not, I fancy, be very far out.

The principal Indian tribes of Manitoba are the Crees, Swampy (Cree), and Chippewa. But among them, members of many other tribes are found, as, for example, Sioux, and Tuskororas. For few if any of the tribes really occupy their old territories, the system of reservation introduced about twenty years ago having changed all that. A distinction is always drawn between *plain* and *forest* Indians. It is not easy to see much difference between them in the North, though the Indian of the lower plains is no doubt of an inferior type. In the old days there was no doubt a difference in habit; the plain Indians living largely on the bison, the forest Indians on fish, birds, and rabbits. But the disappearance of the bison and the Government subsidies have reduced them, on the whole, to a level.

From the recent report of the Mounted Police, it appears that the Indian is showing some signs of improvement in agricultural industries and in

IN THE LAND OF THE GREAT SPIRIT

civilisation generally. But this must be necessarily a very gradual and slow development, and although I can only write of the Indians as I knew them a few years ago, I suspect that the estimate I then formed would on the whole hold good to-day. Among the settlers a proverb obtains to this effect, "God never created any better thing than a dead Indian." My experience is quite opposed to this. The Indian is not bad until he has been spoilt by the whites. I am afraid there is no escaping from this fact, and the story of native races all over the world confirms it. Away out in the lonely forests, away from the towns, away from the ranches, the Indian is not bad. He is grateful, he is not murderous, he is not a thief. If feats of horse-stealing are tests of prowess with the young braves of certain tribes—the Crows, the Bloods, the Blackfeet, for example—does that prove anything? Such feats of daring are points of honour, and as such are fully recognised among those tribes. Petty pilfering is not an Indian's fault. Individual thieves are found in any society. But you may leave your tent open and unguarded by an Indian camp and not a thing will be touched. You may trust yourself alone with the Indians night after night and day after day where no human hand could help you if attacked, and you shall be as safe as in St. James' Street at home. It is so.

But the Indian is quick at reading character. If a white man plays fast and loose with him, if he says one thing and does another, if he treats him as a creature inferior to himself, then there will be trouble. And, without going into particulars, this fact may be taken to explain why, on the whole, we succeed in our management of the Indians, and why, on the whole, the Americans do not.

I think the Indian's power of physical endurance has been overrated. I have hunted with some of the leading Indian hunters of certain districts, and I think an Englishman in training could always wear them down in pace and staying power. But the redskin is very, very lithe. I have by me now an old pair of Hudson Bay Co.'s handcuffs that a London constable would mock at as far too small. And there are three points and three only in which no Englishman I think could ever hope to approach the redskin's skill. In the "homing" instinct, in ability of tracking, in moving silently and rapidly over difficult ground, here he is quite alone, as I think we shall agree when we come to the moose; and we are moving out with this object now.

IN THE LAND OF THE GREAT SPIRIT

Two trackers—Kakikapo, a Cree, and Tiah, a Sioux—an old half-breed who can talk a little French, to cook and be camp-man generally, and a boy, Paupukhi, who seemed to have no tribe, these are our following. Kakikapo and Tiah ride each a pony, there are two light wooden carts drawn by a pony apiece, and an extra baggage pony or two for loading moose-heads, and against emergencies.

We cross a narrow arm of the lake, swimming where we cannot wade, or rather floated over at the ponies' tails. Here the Indians stop to examine their nets. These lakes are full of white fish and pickerel and pike. The white fish * is considered in America one of the very best fish they have. It has no qualities as a sporting fish, but there is no doubt whatever that as a form of food it has most remarkable properties. It seems to be the one form of fish-food upon which human beings can live the whole year through in perfect health. Unfortunately, the great Indian harvest of this species is in autumn, at the spawning time, just when the fish are at their worst as food. Netted then and dried, it is kept for winter use. This fish averages from three to four pounds in weight.

* *Coregonus albus.*

And now we are entering the forest lands. For mile upon mile we trudge on through the region of the balsam poplar, that in spring scents all the air, and at time of seeding floats far and wide a white and downy pappus like soft-falling snow. And now we have left the alluvial flats and are travelling over higher, sandier ground, where the shiver of the aspen sounds even in the stillest hour like a ceaseless, steady rustling breeze, or voices of a million cascades playing somewhere in the hollows out of sight. There is no track here, and so closely grow the aspens that more than once the black pony's packs are swept off his sides as he passes between the trunks. For the black pony is a bit pigheaded, and takes instant advantage of any inattention by running off by himself at a tangent, so that the old half-breed curses him in French and Indian, muttering dire invectives against "Le coureur." Poor Le coureur, we lost him altogether in a bog at last.

For three days we travel so, sleeping by the fire at night and moving off at earliest dawn. But now the evidences of moose begin to grow more frequent. More often do we come upon the great fresh slot in the soft places, more often upon the freshly eaten branches, more often upon the lairs in the grass. So reaching a knoll crowned by a few stunted oak-trees, we go into our first camp.

Snowy Owls and Moose.

Even off-days in camp-life pass very pleasantly. When actually on the hunt the excitement and concentration of attention on the one object leave small room for other studies; but an off-day now and then is absolutely necessary, or the camp would go to pieces. And then, when there is nothing more to be done—when you have finished skinning, mended moccasins, looked to the horses, cleaned up the camp —then is the time to go quietly out among the birds and beasts.

There is no want of animal life in these wild parts. Along the lake-side one morning went flying five white geese with black-tipped wings. The guns were in the tent; but they were probably, like two that we shot later, the smaller snow-goose.* For this bird breeds on the Alaskan peninsula, and as winter approaches moves eastwards across the continent; while the larger species—the "wavy" †— seems rather to follow the coast-line.

* *Chen hypoboreus* (Pal.).   † *Chen albatus.*

Another morning there was a sudden excitement among the Indians, for out of a hole in a stub popped an ermine in winter dress right between their legs as they sat at breakfast.

Our most beautiful visitors perhaps were the snowy owls.* At one place a pair of these birds haunted our camp for a week on end. Often when the Indians were sleeping and the camp was still, and I had gone out to see to the ponies and make the fire up, I could catch a glimpse of these white wanderers sailing along low down in the splendid moonlight. One time I especially remember. It was later on then, and the land lay wrapped in snow. A sound behind the tent awoke me—a scratching, scraping sound. Peeping cautiously round the tent corner, I made it out. Three coyottes were gnawing at a moose's skull and horns which we had that day cleaned and left lying in the snow. I drove them off. There was no moon, but I piled timber on the fire till it blazed again. So I stayed for a space, listening to the sounds of night—the barking of foxes, and the belling of the elk. And as I stood two snowy owls came into view, like great white moths,

* *Nyctea scandiaca* (Linn.).

IN THE LAND OF THE GREAT SPIRIT

attracted by the shining of the light. At least I suppose they were attracted so, for they did not seem to be on the hunt, but only flew backwards and forwards, backwards and forwards, now nearer, now farther off, and sometimes they almost brushed my face. I have never heard these birds make any sound when on the hunt. But this pair, when startled from their resting-place, almost invariably took wing with a loud half-croak, half-wheeze. For they spent all the hours of daylight for several days down on the ground in the scrub by the edge of a lake, and I never saw them hunting during the day. I do not say they never hunt in daylight; no doubt, when pushed for food, they do. But all the snowy owls I saw, and I saw several, were only diurnal in so far as they sat about and occasionally moved from point to point in the daytime.

On November the 25th, driving home from a sleigh journey I saw, at about two o'clock in the day, a snowy owl sitting on a telegraph-post by the side of the high-road not two miles from Winnipeg. I pulled up underneath and sat looking up at him. Judged from below he was, I think, the whitest specimen I ever saw; I could not detect a single spot upon him. He remained there perfectly unconcerned.

He was so beautiful a specimen that I could not resist the temptation to secure him. But the horses, a very spirited pair of trotters, could not be trusted. So I told a half-breed who was with me to shoot. The man took a deliberate pot-shot at the bird, and either missed clean, or else something was wrong with the charge; for the snowy, with a cry of mockery, skimmed grandly off across the flats. The hawk owl,* on the other hand, is diurnal in every sense. It will even sometimes cut down like a peregrine at a wounded spruce partridge.

There need never be a want of food in camp, for the grey hare† is always with you more or less. Some districts literally "crawl" with these creatures. By the beginning of November they are turning white, and lose their colour first up their sides. Any Indian boy can bring in as many of these as you want. For the grey hare is exceedingly stupid. If it hears any sharp sound, a sudden tap or a sharp whistle, it will stop dead and allow its pursuer to come up close enough even to knock it over with a straight-thrown stick.

It would take far too long a time even to quote

* *Syrnia funerea.*   † *L. Americanus.*

from a note-book half the birds and animals met with even in a single day. But I think perhaps some little account of the principal creature we have come out to hunt should not be quite left out. I cannot pretend for a moment that all that follows is the immediate outcome of my own observation. But I think I shall not be found to have stated anything here that is not well ascertained as fact. Statements by the Indians, reports of other hunters, written accounts which I believe to be reliable, and my own observation—these are the sources from which the following is drawn.

The moose* is by far the largest of all the family of the deer. A big bull will measure at the shoulder 72 inches, or, as we should say of a horse, 18 hands. I have never had one weighed, but I have seen it stated somewhere that such an enormous weight as twelve hundred pounds is not unknown, and I can quite believe it. Well, that is more than eighty stone, or, speaking generally, about four times the weight of a fine Highland stag. Readers of Gilbert White will remember how greatly he was struck by the length of the leg (of the tibia especially), the shortness of the

* *Alces Americanus.*

neck, and the prolongation of the upper lip or moufle. And it is just these points that give the moose its quaint and rather ungainly character.

When in the full vigour of life, the bull moose has a curious process of hairy skin some four or five inches long, called the "bell," hanging from its throat. It is not believed that this functions as a gland. I have heard that this is also occasionally seen on females, but I never remember to have myself seen one that had it. The colour of the moose is very variable, but always in some tone of black or grey. I have never seen the slightest tinge of red in any adult.

There is by me as I write a magnificent robe or skin which has not been stretched at all. Kakikapo's squaw prepared it, scraping it clean with an old axe-head and tanning it in the smoke of the wood-fire. This skin measures from the scut to the front of the withers eight feet six.

Its colour is a beautiful glistening black, with here and there the slightest suspicion of grey. But this is the early winter skin of a bull in his prime. Later on in the year this coat would have turned grey. Females and young are grey, and very old males incline even to white. A second small skin, also in my possession, which I believe to be the skin of a fawn of this species (the Indian from whom I obtained it assured me it was), may be thus described: Sides and shoulders the dark sable-brown of the British water-vole. A stripe three inches broad of lighter sable down the back, widening over the quarters and fading to chestnut towards the hocks. From the neck to the lumbar region down the centre of the back a dark mule-mark. This skin measures from the origin of the neck to the end of the scut twenty-six inches, and is thirteen inches wide across the flanks.

The palmated horns of the moose are too well known to need description. They are shed about mid-winter. The coat is shed twice—viz., in May and September. The rutting season, which begins in September, is at its height by October, and the calves are dropped in May.

Unlike the wapiti, or our red-deer, the moose is monogamous, although the bull seems to pair with a different cow each season. Each family holds together through the year, so that a big bull is not often found alone, unless his powers are going back.

The moose, because of his long fore-legs, can only eat grass with great difficulty. Personally I have never seen any evidence of their eating grass at all, and probably they seldom do in the natural state, except perhaps in summer when the grasses are long. But Gilbert White's account of the Duke of Richmond's female moose (1768) is worth quoting on this point:

"With this length of legs, its neck was remarkably short, no more than twelve inches; so that by straddling with one foot forward and the other backward it grazed on the plain ground, with the greatest difficulty between its legs." A colt does the same.

It ordinarily feeds on leaves and twigs. A very favourite food is the red dog-wood, called by the Indian "*kinikinik.*" (It is the dried bark of this shrub that the Indians smoke, instead of or mixed with tobacco.) In winter, you will often come upon a large area in which every tree has been barked by the moose. And you will find many spruce-trees whose young shoots have been bitten off by the creature to an astonishing height from the ground. They must raise themselves on their hind feet in order to accomplish this. But the very fact of their eating spruce at all is curious. Turpentine is, so far as my observation goes, avoided by almost all animals except squirrels.

In winter the moose have a well-known habit of congregating together and forming a yard, probably for the purpose of protection from wolves. These yards have been often described as if almost made with the accuracy and precision of a Danish camp—as being perfect even-sided entrenchments. I have never had the good fortune to see the animals in their yard. But one of the so-called yards themselves I have seen. Of a most irregular and imperfect formation, situated in the closest part of the forest, it showed no features that would not naturally result from a number of large animals being collected together in one place. The snow, trampled down and scraped together here and there, lent some colour to the idea of a fortification, but that was all. Irregular paths ran from this centre for a short distance in many directions, and this plan or principle (if so it can be called) was always traceable in the yards of the previous year one came across in the autumn. For old yards are easily recognised, because every bush and twig has been killed down by the moose. The caribou is said to have the same habit, but to this I cannot speak.

Moose are killed in various ways. Sometimes they are taken by the Indians by means of a noose and running block fixed up in the paths along which they travel. Again, in time of deep snow when, under the influence of the sun and frost, the snow is covered with a hard skin, the Indian hunters, and I am sorry to say others also, pursue them on snow-shoes. The hard surface of the snow bears the hunter well enough, but the moose, sinking deep at every plunge and cut about the legs by the knife-edge of the ice, soon succumbs and is despatched. Indians, I have heard, also kill the moose in the water when he goes in summer to bathe and feed on lily roots.

But all these are contemptible and most unsportsman-like ways. There are only two plans, so far as I am aware, which can be classed as honest sport—that is, if judged by the only test which a sportsman should admit—viz., difficulty and the fair outwitting the wild creature by skill alone. The first is the call. This is, they say, much practised in Nova Scotia, chiefly in the early half of the rutting season. The bull is attracted to the hunter by a call blown on a trumpet of birch-bark. Everything here depends on an intimate knowledge of the animal's habits and of the perfect imitation of its voice—a most difficult accomplishment. I have never seen it done, but it must in the moonlit night be most exciting work.

But no form of moose-hunting, I think, is worthy to be compared with still-hunting. The still-hunt must make greater demands upon a man's power of endurance, readiness of resource, knowledge of animal habit, quickness of sight, with all the other qualities that go to make the success of the big-game hunter, than all the other methods put together.

The particular hunt that follows has not been chosen because it was one of the most successful, for indeed it ended badly. Moose hunts sometimes do, and this was only the third moose I had seen.

We have all heard and read of the man who never misses. Have you ever met him personally? I never have, and perhaps I never shall. But I know this, that big as the moose is, it is easily possible to miss it. And the instance that follows is a case in point. After all, the interest of a hunt lies not always, nor chiefly, in the kill; and this, full though it was of disappointment, was a very memorable hunt.

A Still Hunt.

Just a sense of coming day was beginning to feel over the forest as Kakikapo and I left camp. We rose at first a gradual hill covered with white shining poplar, and then dropped down to a land of black spruce and scrub and " muskegs " or bogs.

Kakikapo cut a comical figure. An old grey shirt, a pair of trousers made in the Hudson Bay Co.'s best manner, moccasins, round his waist a red and blue "ascension" scarf into which his fire-bag was tucked, at his back an old meat-tin for boiling tea in, and a single-barrelled gun—these were his leading features.

To-day it seemed we really were in luck. For less than thirty yards along the muskeg's edge we came upon a slot—an immense slot, and apparently no other near it. For me this was enough. It was a perfectly fresh track, the merest tyro could have told that; it was the track of a big bull, and it pointed right into the wind. What more could we possibly want? I re-tied my moccasins with great care, I slipped in the cartridges, I was ready to move on. But Kakikapo was not ready yet. Along the side of the muskeg he walked some fifty yards or so and back on either hand. And then he came back, looking puzzled, and stopped to think. This was perhaps how his reasoning went. "This is the foot of a big bull. But he is alone. Where is his cow? He should be paired by now. Is he an old supplanted bull? If so, we lose time by following him. He will have no head. Is he a travelling bull? If so, is it worth while to follow him? How comes he so near our camp? Have our shots or voices frightened him? What pace is he going? Let us see." The Cree's reflections evidently brought him to some such point as this, for now he began following on the spoor.

It took us straight to the middle of the muskeg. Here was a large piece of open water, and this the moose had crossed. That a creature of the moose's enormous weight can easily cross the softest bogs has always been a wonder to me. But he does it. His great splay feet bear him up sufficiently. But you, if by any carelessness you should step in a moose's footprint, find your own leg dropped three feet into a hole from which you have much ado again to clear it.

But there was nothing for it now but to retrace our steps. "Nipi" (water), said the Cree, and there was no denying that. So back we went, and round the muskeg till we came at last on that point where the creature had come out. And then away into the forest the great slot led. He had stopped a little further on, had done a little feeding on the kinikinik, and then had moved on more slowly right through a thick grove of larches. And here, right and left, and very high up, were the broken branches, and once in passing between two trees quite wide apart he had scraped right and left with his horns. He had horns then, and, goodness, what a width they must have been! No wonder Kakikapo put his gun down here, drew himself up slowly to his full height, stretched out his arms on either side his head, and said impressively below his breath, "*Tcheh* api"—*big* bull.

Following a moose is a serious matter, and nothing is gained by hurry. We had had breakfast before daylight, and now it was half-past ten. So we drew off a little down the wind, lit a tiny fire, and made some tea in Kakikapo's tin, while he munched at his dried moose-meat, I at a luncheon biscuit. And then the Cree almost undressed and dressed himself again. I can see him now, hitching here, tying there; he seemed all strings and patches. But the result was satisfactory to himself. Not a loop, not a loose end anywhere, nothing that could catch a twig or make the slightest noise. And then he looked me over. I had put on that day over my grey shirt for the first time a jacket bought at a Hudson Bay Fort. It seemed just the thing, for it was made of yellowish canvas lined with cloth. Its colour, that so exactly matched the dead grasses, pleased me very much. But Kakikapo was not pleased. For he picked a little twig and brushed it across my sleeve, and sure enough that noise, though slight, was more than we could risk when after moose. I turned the jacket inside out, and then all was ready; and we began to take that spoor along.

The breeze, so very light when we started, had freshened up and was now blowing pretty strong. And this perhaps was just as well, for about twelve o'clock we entered upon a bit of hunting just about as difficult as anything I have ever come across. We had all but come upon our moose. But he had begun to suspect something was wrong. Whiskey Jack, I fancy, put the notion in his head. A word or two before I forget it about Whiskey Jack.

There is a little grey bird with a black head whose place is somewhere between the jays and shrikes. His proper name is *Perisoreus canadensis*, but to the Indian he is known as Wiskachan; and thence passes, by an easy transition in settler language, through Whiskey John to Whiskey Jack. This little bird is most sociably disposed towards human beings. Some Whiskey Jack of days gone by made the grand discovery that, when hunters stopped and lit a fire, there was commonly food about. This information spread through all the forest lands of the Territory; and now, when any hunter stops for food, it is ten chances to one that, before he has finished his first hunch of bread, Whiskey Jack will be there, with one or two more, to see him eat it and help him through. So amazing is the audacity of this bird that, when there is time to spare, it may be drawn nearer and nearer by well-considered devices, until it makes bold to snatch food from the hand itself, as on one occasion it snatched it from mine. But W. Jack's ways are not all prettiness. For, like our English jay, he is a terrible alarmist in the woods.

Whether or not it was he that put the big bull on the look-out it is impossible to say, but the creature began to grow suspicious and took to walking in semi-circles, trying to get our wind. It was a curious performance. Now and then we heard him, more often we only saw the slot. We tried hard to head him at his points. But no sooner did we begin to draw up to him than he would turn again and come right round on the other side. If he had once fairly winded us, he would have gone. But he never did. Only now and then he thought he caught some half scent or heard some doubtful sound, and, besides, the wind made him uneasy, for he could not listen well. We dared not go straight on, or we should soon have had him on our flank and all would have been up.

Excepting the fact that the growth was very thick, nothing could well have been worse for us. For over large areas here and there the bush had been broken down some time, and lay, so to say, a thick stratum of "spelicans." Through this we had to pick our way, lifting at each step the foot over some obstructing bough and feeling carefully down among the dry branches against any twig that might be lying in the moss, before one dared to trust one's weight on something that might snap. At this game the Cree surpassed me altogether. Over and over again he forged ahead and disappeared from view. We never saw the bull, but for five hours by my watch this game of hide-and-seek went on. And then at last the moose seemed satisfied and began to draw straight on. And now the wind, blowing half a gale, was all in our favour, for we were out again in open country, only kinikinik and willow patches here and there and the rest all bog and grass. Right on through the willows the moose had passed, feeding on the young shoots as he went. Presently we passed through a belt of larches, and there lay before us a flat open tract of white grass high as the knee, over which the wind came rolling like waves upon the sea. Through this on hands and knees we crept very, very warily.

About every two hours a moose lies down. He usually begins to move irregularly when he is thinking of resting, and often comes back a little and throws off, as it were, a bit to the side, and there he makes his bed. He likes just such a place as this for his siesta, and at any moment now our moose might be springing to his feet. But no. Straight on went the track, and then, when about seventy yards from the edge of the covert, inch by inch we raised ourselves on our hands and looked. Shall I ever forget it? Never.

Immediately opposite us was a small point covered thick with willow scrub. Behind this an impenetrable background of black spruce fir-trees and of golden larch. And there, topping the foremost willow-bush of all, were two gigantic horns. That was the first impression, *gigantic*. To me it seemed indeed the veritable head of an Irish elk, so long was the beam, so wide apart the extreme ends of the antlers. The moose's head was raised to its full height, and straight at us he looked. I could see his neck, I could see his chest; his body was out of sight, his legs were hid by the willow. It was a great moment.

Well, I was a fool. I was new then at the work, and did the wrong thing. Slowly I rolled over on my back and round till my feet were towards the moose. Then, little by little, I raised myself, and aiming at the point where the neck meets the chest, I fired. For the space of a moment there was no result. Then the moose swung round, and as he turned I fired again at his shoulder. He dropped, recovered himself, and crashed into the forest. A hurried inspection showed that the first ball had touched a willow twig and turned. What had the second done?

We followed up to see. There was blood along the track, and the moose was going on three legs. Surely he could not travel very far like that, we thought, and in that belief we hunted on.

But it takes a good deal to stop a moose, and twilight found us still pursuing. With the last gleam of the sunset we had come to the side of a smallish muskeg. In the middle was a bit of open water, and near it lay a fallen tree, its bare roots all sharp against the whitening water. Nothing could be done by going on that night; we decided to stop and try to make out something in the morning. As we stood for a moment listening, for the wind had dropped, Kakikapo suddenly drew my attention to a sound that came from across the swamp. It was, as I heard it, very, very slight. I think I should not have noticed it at all but for the Cree. He described a circle on the ground with his hand and said softly "moose," meaning that a moose was making his bed. It seems very wonderful now, but I believed him, and still feel certain he was right. But suddenly, while I was listening and trying to make this out, another incident befell that one could not choose but understand. Crash! smash! as though two giants fought with willow trees for clubs. Two bull moose were charging one another in the bush—well, certainly not a hundred yards away. I picked up my rifle and was moving off. It was almost dark, but it would surely be easy enough to follow to that sound. But Kakikapo protested with signs and mutterings, "It was too dark. I should never see them. I should spoil all. The first thing to-morrow morning we should go." Well, I weighed chances. Most reluctantly I resigned the chance of seeing a fight between two bull moose. But resign it I did.

So we drew off down wind some half a mile or so, and then by the edge of the muskeg, in a hollow where a tree had some time grown, we made a fire, and dried our moccasins in the smoke.

We had no tea left, but Kakikapo finished his dried moose meat, and I, who had nothing to eat, smoked my pipe. The Cree prepared some kinikinik in the usual way. Taking a piece of the young wood, he skinned off the red outer bark and then scraped the inner bark till it formed a frill round the stick like the paper frill of a ham. This, stuck in front of the fire, was soon dry enough for smoking. But it was slow work watching Kakikapo blinking at the fire, and I could not get those fighting moose out of my thoughts. It struck me that possibly in the morning they might come down to drink, so I took my rifle and crept off in the darkness till I found the fallen tree, and there I lay, comfortably enough for a bit, out of the wind behind the big uplifted roots. But things went wrong.

I had fallen asleep, and awoke at 11.30 to hear the muttering of thunder. It looked black and threatening, and a storm was evidently coming on. Creeping back I woke up Kakikapo and made him understand the need of shelter. Very reluctantly he moved, but at length muttering "pineah" (pine-trees), he led the way. I remembered having seen the pine-trees, they were right across the swamp. Before we had gone a hundred yards the storm burst upon us and the rain came down in torrents. By each lightning flash we ran as far as we could see and then waited for the next. For a muskeg is not a good place to walk in in the dark. Several times we dropped a leg into moose-foot holes, and had a wretched scramble to get out. But at any rate it ended amusingly for me. For the Cree, in making his final effort on the other side, tumbled bang into something that looked like an elder-bush, and sat down in the middle of it swearing Indian oaths. I roared with laughter, it was so comical, and this made him worse. However, at last we reached the pineah, and there we spent a most unpleasant night. We were literally wet to the skin, and could only find an odd spruce twig or so that was dry enough to light. But we slept at last, and woke to find the storm gone, the sky clear, and a sharp white frost. This was bad and delayed us for some hours, for it was hopeless to think of a still hunt with the grass and leaves dry and crackling. So I filled up the time by picking berries, cranberries, and "muskegomin," or bog-cranberries, and made what meal I could.

There is little more to add. We found the place where the fight had taken place, and a wonderful mess it had made. Broken branches torn-up ground, lumps of hair lying all about. We did not follow the animals, but took up the old spoor. We felt pretty certain that our big bull would be too stiff to travel much, and that sooner or later we should bring him to book. And this we should have done but for an untimely performance on the part of the Cree. It fell on this wise.

The bull was still trying to travel. But not being pushed, he took it as easily as he could, lying down at frequent intervals. Closer and closer we drew upon him, and about twelve o'clock there were unmistakable evidences that he was not far off. I had hung back for a moment to tighten a moccasin. Kakikapo in front, by some unaccountable carelessness, caught his toe in a stump or something, fell forward, and in recovering swung round the stock of his gun, which hit upon the tin he carried at his back with a loud clash. Instantly there was a crash in the bushes as the big bull, who had been lying down not forty yards away, rose and went pounding off among the trees.

It was a sad journey home and a weary one, for nothing tires like disappointment.

But I shot my first great grey owl* that evening by

* *Syrnia cinerea.*

a device of Kakikapo. For the owl flew from top to top of the pine-trees as often as I tried to approach. Whereupon the Cree hid in the grass and, squeaking like a rat, threw his cap away in front of him. Down on to this the owl pounced, and I dropped him as he was carrying it off.

For we did not reach the camp till dark, and I got back pretty hungry.

But that was the end of Tcheh Api.

IN NORFOLK BY THE SEA

IN NORFOLK BY THE SEA

On the east coast of Norfolk lies a little town whose people, for rough manners with good intentions, are distinct from any in England. There is nothing worse than this about them, and very much that is better. Their town is charming,

It is set in a little from the sea—lying there with its back to the cornfields and its face to a waste of marsh. But at flood the sea makes in by the creek, lifting the boats that lie upon the mud-banks and lapping against the stones of the little quay. The town, with its couple of big windmills and its long low line of wharves and old red-tiled houses, looks very, very Dutch. From the sea-front inwards it is bisected by a series of long passages which, sometimes approached by an arched entry bored through the houses, begin by being extremely narrow, but end by being fairly wide—begin as "yards" and end as streets. The commerce of this seaboard has moved westward now, and a hundred years ago the town, they say, was nearly twice as big. But this merely means that the population has fallen from four thousand souls to little more than half that number, not that the town is any smaller than it was. It covers the same area; only many of the houses are coming, as many have come, down. And it is this growth of open spaces that gives the town much of its peculiar charm. For up and down the streets are high walls pierced with doorways through which you glance in passing, prepared to see the squalor of a court. But instead of this the eye strikes in on gardens ablaze with roses and honeysuckle, and touched with every shade of green. So—and strangely for a society centred on cockles and mussels—its kitchen middens are kept out of sight.

And these means to existence are always with it— the mussels brought in and formed in beds, the cockles picked up when any tide is low. For its people are not ambitious; they have come to realise that happiness lies not in gain of hard-earned money, but rather in ease and contemplation; a philosophy which they owe perhaps to the School Board. Even as the old harbour-oracle, asked one day for his opinion about education, with slow emphasis defined it

IN NORFOLK BY THE SEA

thus: "*My* 'pinion? My 'pinion is this. Eddication is *schemin' to live without warkin'*."

The land all round is rich in suggestions of the Danes. A little way inland lies a Danish camp, as perfect—its double bank, its double ditch, and its three causeways—as perfect now as in those first days when the old raider kept sentry there and watched the surrounding country with eyes as keen as the hawk's. Only now the creek up which he brought his ships is narrowed to a trout-stream; only now the chalk is thick with grasses in which the titlark makes its nest.

For either by natural processes or under the reclaiming hand of man, tidal creeks everywhere traceable have been dried or silted up. And here where the ships rode at the foot of another camp there once survived a bit of fresh water used as a decoy pond; and still it keeps the name. But the fruit-trees of the decoy-men's garden have long gone back to a wild condition, and the big pond has shrunk to a little swampy hollow where the nest of the reed-warbler swings in the sedge. And here is a shallow brackish mere that still fills by narrow ditches when the tide runs in, where the wildfowl lie quiet from storm and billow. And the mere is known as "Jacob's Rest."

It is not at every tide that the little vessels which venture here can get in or out of the harbour. And often a grain-bearing Danish schooner will be a month or more just off the point, tried by the local tug from time to time, for even at the spring tides there is little more than twelve feet of water by the quay. And a mile or so out seawards round the point stretches a long sand and shingle bar on which many a good craft has gone to pieces. But if there must be wrecks, then wrecks are very welcome here, for they bring a little easy money to the town. Inside the bar at low water is a fine expanse of ooze, then the long line of the sandhills, and closer in the marsh.

The marshes are never so dreary even in wild winter-time but that they have one great abiding charm, their beauty of bird-life. For in winter the place is alive with wildfowl, with casual small parties of bean and white-fronted geese, and with pink-footed geese in thousands from the polar seas, while Iceland sends a contingent of snow-white hooper swans, moving away down south. By March the scene is changed. Only some belated widgeon or shoveller and the home proportion of mallards remain, but from then on till the middle of May there are daily arrivals of birds moving northwards to nest. Golden plover, grey plover, small groups of whimbrel, an occasional reeve—these and many others, in varying states of plumage, drop in from day to day. But by about the first week of June things have settled down pretty well into their places. And it is any day in this first week of June that we are now to spend with a field-glass out among the sandhills, seeing a little of all there is to see.

It is easy now the tide is running down to get out in a small boat to the eastern point. An old man takes us there who has been a notable gunner in his day. He is full of quaint old memories, and is most anxious to get an opinion on the nature of some wonderful bird he met with one night or early morning on his way back from the flats. But his description is vague. This is it. "I thought as I could hear somethin' a biblin', and, before I could get my gun up, that scouted, and went off like a shimmer of ice. That did, bor," repeats the old man with serious emphasis, "that went off like a *shimmer of ice*."

But this is "the Point"; the point, that is, of the eastern sandhills, where they sink first to broken tufts of grasses and then to a shingle bed. About this shingle are nesting some twenty pairs or so of little terns.* They arrived, perhaps from the Mediterranean, in the middle of last month and laid their first eggs on the 26th. They are not shy, and lying here in the grass it is easy enough to watch their ways. At first they circle round and round, uttering all the while the chiding note from which they get the local name of "chits" or "chit perles"; a "perle" being a tern. But soon they return to their several duties, the female settling down on to her eggs, the male sitting by or coasting off to look for food, now skimming swallow-like up the creek, now hanging poised like a kestrel on vibrating wings, to drop like an arrow into the water and take a fish.† And then follows often a performance which must be described somewhat particularly because it does not seem to be noticed in the books.

Returned from its quest, the bird with a fish in its bill circles round and round and lower and lower over its mate, and presently drops down beside her.

* *Tringa minuta.*

† I have assumed these sexes from the birds' behaviour only. I do not know that the male takes any share in hatching of eggs. As a matter of fact, closely as sexes may resemble each other—as in this case—it is always, I think, possible to determine them from habits.

Then he begins a series of extraordinary evolutions. With head thrown back, wings drooping, and tail cocked straight up, he struts—no other word expresses it—he struts about in front of his mate. The attitude, a most comical one, is exactly that assumed by the "laughing jackass" kingfisher when laughing. He jumps at his mate as if daring her to take the fish. Then he will fly round for a bit only to settle again and repeat the play. I have seen on several occasions a female "chit," before she has settled down on her eggs, get up, fly off, settle on the shingle off and on for a considerable time, followed persistently by her fish-bearing partner, but always avoiding him as if coqueting or really annoyed. Sooner or later the fish is either relinquished or, as I suspect, taken by the female bird, though this I have not seen.

One is led at first to wonder how the rabbits which swarm in these sandhills can manage to thrive without any water to drink. For there is no fresh water within their reach, and it is clear that they cannot drink the salt water of the tidal creeks. But the rabbit is not, perhaps, by nature a creature that requires much water, and doubtless its wants are sufficiently supplied by dew and the juices of the herbage. At the same time, the extent to which animals can adapt themselves to adverse circumstances is sometimes very remarkably shown. Thus it is a matter of common observation in this country that rats and mice are among the very thirstiest of creatures. Yet it is well known that a race of mice supports itself and thrives among the stones of the Egyptian desert. And Darwin long ago remarked how "in Patagonia, even on the borders of the salinas, where a drop of fresh water can never be found, excepting dew, these little animals swarm."*

From the foot of the sandhills right away to the creek by the town stretches the waste of marsh, which at the high spring tides is greatly under water. There was a time† when much of this was under cultivation. But the sea found out a weak place in the sandhills and flooded in; yet still the remains of ridge and furrow can be plainly seen.

Many and varied are the flowers that grow upon the marsh. In the softer places grows the glasswort ‡—the favourite food of the mallard—and everywhere, where the grass is short and dry, the

---

* *Journal of Researches*, Edition 1890, p. 384

† Probably during the great war, when wheat fetched 100s. a quarter.

‡ *Salicornia herbacea*

beautiful little pink sea-glaux. Here are acres and acres gay with thrift and green with the strong leaves of the common sea-lavender. And another sea-lavender is there, one with matted, net-like leaves and white bracts to its flowers.* All about in this the common terns nest, as well as on the low tables of the sandhills, in the wrack along high-water line, and in the scratchings of the rabbits which swarm about the hills. They make slightly more pretence at a nest perhaps, than do the little terns; not only dropping in the bits of shell, but often fringing the cup round with bents and bits of seaweed, or anything else that comes easily to hand.

But the terns have so many foes that often they are sore put to it to bring their young ones off. In spite of all efforts at protection the boys sometimes will leave their cockle-gathering to slip up over the bank and take the eggs. In a dry season, too, when food is scarce the rooks are dreaded visitors. If a rook can settle at once and not lose his head, he can walk from nest to nest and pilfer finely, for the terns, though they fly round and cry, do not touch him then. But

* *Statice reticulata.* There are but two other English counties—Suffolk and Cambridge—in which this plant is found.

once on the wing and it is a different story. Down at him drop the terns one after another, stooping and cutting at him till they beat him off. And even the big herring gulls when they fly over are followed far and mobbed by the terns. But there is one foe with which the terns sometimes forget to reckon, and this foe is the tide. It happens by a timely dispensation that the smallest spring tides in all the year fall just at nesting-time, so that they are called the "bird-tides" in this place. But, low by comparison as they are, even so they sometimes catch many eggs, foolishly laid on the lowest spots.

Lucky indeed it is for the terns that the arch-robber, the hoodie crow (called here the "Densh," *i.e.* the Danish crow), is absent now. It is in autumn and winter that the hoodie comes to feed on the big mussels smashed by being dropped on the stones from a height.

Many of the little green crabs that sidle round in the creeks lose their lives to this bandit crow. These little crabs have queer quaint ways well worth the studying if we had but time. We shall cross several small creeks as we go to the sandhills from the marsh, and there one cannot but notice how the crabs travel from point to point in beaten tracks. Here, where the mud is dry and cracked, these little crab-paths are well defined. And there in all likelihood they will now remain until the end of time. For the tides that follow will each in its turn lay over the track a deposit of mud from the washings of the muddy banks. And then as time goes on, and pressure is added and clay-stone formed, and the land raised up perhaps above the sea-level—well, then, hundreds of thousands of years hence, an old professor may come with his hammer and lecture on these remarkable crustacean evidences. Why should it not be so? It has happened before. The very oldest tracks known (they are there in the Cromwell Road) are those of a crab allied to Limulus the king crab, who had a tail which dragged. And because he lived so early and made as he walked even little impressions on either side of his tail-mark, they named him *Protichnites septemnotatus*, though no actual remains of him have ever been seen, or had not when Sir Richard Owen wrote the facts which I have given.

Over there, where the sandhills are planted with various kinds of pine, a pair of thick-knee or Norfolk plover * nested this year, for the first time on record.

* *Œdicnemus scolopax* (Gmelin).

This bird, quite apart from its own very quaint appearance and habits, must always have a great interest for British ornithologists, as it is the nearest surviving link we have with the great bustard, now, alas! extinct in this country. It is nocturnal in its habits, and is extremely wary and shy. Although on its arrival in spring it keeps well away in the open, it generally lays its eggs not far from a covert or belt of trees. The pair of which I speak had chosen the middle of a gravelly space among the pines. By creeping up on hands and knees under cover of a bank one could gain a position, just fifteen paces away from the nest, without being observed: so close that with my glass I could see the light shine through the crystal prominence of the sitting bird's great yellow eyes. At intervals one bird would relieve the other on the nest. When disturbed the birds always ran for shelter to a bank beneath the pines. And here the bird that was not sitting always stood as sentry. When its turn came to relieve its mate it would walk pretty deliberately across the first part of the open, where it was more or less screened by a fringe of trees; and there,. having reached a point that was commanded from a long way off, it would suddenly lower its head and run as fast as a red-leg to the nest. When it was about a yard away the sitting bird would slip off and, staying for no greetings, run past and away to the pine-bank. Though I watched these birds for many hours on several days, I never but once saw any change in this procedure. It was interesting to notice that the bird alway rose backwards off the eggs, so that its long legs should not disturb the eggs; and that the newcomer did not turn the eggs immediately, but squatted perfectly still for perhaps a minute, as if to make sure it was not observed. And after the eggs were satisfactorily bestowed, and all the coast seemed clear, the bird would close its eyes in the hot sunshine and appear to go to sleep. But even then I could scarce move so much as a finger above the grasses, but instantly it was off its nest and away.

I never but once heard these birds make their well-known night-call, and that was in the daytime, and before they had fairly begun to sit. But they often made another little noise—a short, clear note of warning. And so I tried experiments, crawling round to another point from which the nest was out of sight, but from which I could see the sentry bird standing at its post. Then I could make never so slight a movement but with that the watcher gave his quiet piping call, the first sound of which sufficed to lure the sitting bird away.

And as they stood together on the bank, it was curious to see the different behaviour of the two. For the bird whose turn it was to sit was all anxiety; walking irresolutely a few feet or so and back, ruffling its feathers, looking eagerly out in the direction of the nest, evidently unable to shake itself together for the passage of that open ground. But the other took a different line; standing still and preening its feathers, and giving its partner a dab of the beak from time to time, as if to say "Hurry up, now; what a nervous fidget you are! Those our two eggs will be getting quite cold."

Is it not marvellous that any plant, not being a cactus, should find life and growth in this dry sand? Yet many do. The vigorous little sea-purslane* gets a footing anywhere; elder-bushes flourish and flower finely, and make good hiding for the brown linnets' nests; deadly nightshade in rank tufts points to where a hut has some time stood; maram grasses and glaucous blue-grass bind the sands together with their roots.

And now in the very pulse of the sun where it

* *Arenaria peploides.*

beats upon the sandhills we will lie with the glass for a last long look.

Look eastward over the sea. By sunset this evening there will be nothing there but a single distant tower and a thin low line of coast. But now, in the quivering heat, the mirage has lifted the tower up high against the sky, has brought into view the craft lying hidden in the pool, and changed the thin coast-line into lofty cliffs.

The breeze, for all the heat, is blowing in our faces from the north. Yes, in our faces; for look straight out to sea and you are looking north. More than that. Look out and try to realise that, excepting the blue sea, there lies absolutely nothing between yourself and the white lands of the Polar world. The map will tell you there are but three places on our eastern English coast of which this saying could be true; and this is one of the three. The blue sea—the ships upon its bosom—the white wings of the wandering gulls—and then the first awakening of that short summer that lies about the borders of the everlasting ice.

The glass cannot, alas! show us this, but it does make our watch more interesting. A small group of birds sitting out there on the mud are seen to be shelducks, called also "burrowing" ducks, from the habit of their nesting. For this bird nests underground, usually in one of the rabbit-holes of the sandhills. With its crimson bill, and gay magpie and chestnut plumage, it is a very beautiful bird. It is not always safe to conclude that every rabbit-hole which betrays the tracks of the shelduck holds a nest, for the birds usually try several burrows before making a final choice. But by lying down like this, especially at early morning when the sitting bird has been off to feed, it is only too easy to follow her to her nest; too easy, because in this way the eggs are found and stolen. And of those birds now out there on the ooze, only one or two are males whose ducks are sitting, the remainder are pairs who have lost their eggs and have not yet gone again to nest. But at least one brood got off successfully on June 1st, and they are now busy chasing insects in the quiet of "Jacob's Rest." At a week or so old these little black and white ducklings are most accomplished divers, able when alarmed to travel under water for many yards. No haven more perfect for young water-fowl could possibly be found than this peaceful bit of shallow water, where scarce a human being passes, but only the nesting redshank runs piping along the cattle-rails, and glorious marsh orchis* makes crimson all the grass.

But the summer day is drawing to its close. Two months hence the story will again be changed. Even earlier than that the sea-lavender will make of all the marsh an amethystine sea. And then going south again will come the nesting parties of the birds—godwits, knots, stints, curlew-sandpipers, and all their following—some already putting on their winter plumage, but many still in summer dress.

And so will wear the season on until once more the winter falls and brings again the whistling swans.

* *Orchis latifolia.*

THE WITCH IN KENT

THE WITCH IN KENT

LYING, as it does, almost under the shadow of the great metropolis, whither the excursion train will carry a labourer's family from its remotest corner at the price of the wages of a single day, Kent at any rate, it might have been thought, would have been the first to free itself from the hold of a superstition whose doom was sounded long ago. None the less, faith in witchcraft, if dying, is not dead, and some may perhaps find interest in a contemporary record, compiled from the material afforded by one small country parish only, of one phase of its decay.

As far as one can gather, there has never been a time when this parish was without its witch; and, though there is only one now, a generation ago there were three, if not four, women in it all credited with strange powers. If the superstition takes here a milder form than that which exerts so baneful an influence on the Devonshire poor, the difference is one only of degree. "I says to him," remarked a woman to me not long ago who had been having a difference with her son on the subject, "I says to him, 'Doant you blef your *Book*, then? You knowd the Book says as there *were* witches; yes, and wizards too; and as it was in the beginning, it says, it is now and ever shall be.'"

Many were the evils laid at the door of Mother Becket, who, as the folk will tell you, "did just lead them sad lives as she used to terrify." For witches (and the reflection is not without comfort) have not the power of terrifying—*i.e.* troubling—everybody; their power is limited. It was a real relief to the afflicted when Mother Becket retired to a neighbouring almshouse, where, a very old woman, she is living still. Before her retirement, however, while she was still able to get about, one of her victims found release in the following manner. The malevolence of this witch displayed itself in the death or illness of the cattle, poultry, or other animals of those who had incurred it, and one day—but let the writer's informant speak for himself. "Faather, he used to take in ship for Mr. Smith. One day when he comes in to breakfast he says to mother, he says, 'Mother, Mr. Smith's black ship *has* got just a pretty little lamb; I don't know as ever I *did* see one *quite* so pretty; 'tis all over curls.' Well, he hadn't been gone out again not *ten minutes* afore back he comes running. 'Mother,' he says, 'give me the knife quick; Dame Becket's got at that lamb; he's a-lying on his back now a-kickin' his legs up.' Faather, he run out with the knife, and cut that lamb's head off *quick*, he did. You blef Dame Becket went off to the doctor with a *hem an' all* bad throat, and she didn't terrify *him* no more. You see, sir," adds my informant, by way of explanation, "you see, sir, he killed that *afore* it was dead." But the force of the instance lies in the fact that it illustrates a prevalent belief that witches have the power of entering into animals, and that by destroying or wounding the thing possessed, you in some measure weaken *them*.

Akin to this idea, but distinct from it, is another—namely, that it is a common resource with witches to change themselves into animals. A dog (usually a "spannel dog"), an owl, a hare—many are the forms of metamorphosis, the last perhaps the commonest. You will be told of a hare running in and out among the haymakers as they sit at dinner, and of how they all try to hit it, but in vain; and "they know what *that* means," and know, too, that if they strike it without drawing blood they will have to suffer for it; but that should they draw blood, ever so little, "she won't trouble *them* no more."

Barely forty years since there lived in the parish an elderly woman, who had built herself a little furze hut in a lonely field which lies in among the woods. She was a witch. One day, when the men were rabbiting, the dogs started a hare. They followed this hare all day, and finally ran it into Mother Smith's hut and killed it there. The story goes on to say that from that day the witch was never seen again. Probably no very searching inquiry would have been made, for she was "a bad un," and had given a lot of trouble in her time. This field has long been called "The Terrible Downs," and the reputation of its mysterious inhabitant owed, no doubt, not a little to the name and the isolation of her abode. Less mysterious, if more tragic, is the end of another witch at a still more recent date, who was found in bed with her throat cut. No one was ever brought to justice for the crime, though local suspicion pointed to one of whom it was well known that she used to "terrify" him a great deal, and that he had lost many animals "along o' her."

THE WITCH IN KENT

A few years ago the child of a labourer in a cottage hard by was subject to chronic fits. A neighbour—a gardener by profession—was describing to me the symptoms. "And the doctor doesn't seem to do him any good?" I asked. "No," said the man with an expressive jerk of his thumb, as he sank his voice to a whisper, "no, and no doctor *wunt* do him no good; *she's overlooked him.*" "She" in this case was the person upon whom the mantle of the weird woman I have spoken of may be supposed to have fallen; in other words, the present witch. The mention of this woman naturally suggests the question, "How far does she herself lay claim to strange powers? Does she by her profession or practices lend any colour to the popular belief?" The answer, disappointing as it may be, just emphasises the point in its decline at which witchcraft has arrived. I have known this person for many years, and she is, for any evidence I have been able to collect to the contrary, a hard-working, straight-going old woman. It is true she possesses those qualities of *savoir faire* which make her services desirable at births and deaths, and is a proficient in the art of herbs and simples. But beyond this, and the fact that she has a strong individuality and much force of character, which would naturally give her an ascendency over many of her neighbours, I can discover nothing. None the less a witch she is, if local testimony may be believed. Not long ago a young man whose child was given to screaming at night, unable to explain it in any other way, became convinced it was bewitched. Thenceforward he kept his razor by him at night, as a weapon of attack, fully persuaded that, could he only strike a light sufficiently quickly when the screaming began, he should find our witch standing in his room. Prevention, however, is better than cure, and those who are much troubled keep a prayer-book under their pillow, a thing a witch cannot abide. Witches, apparently, do read the Bible, but they read it backwards—a fact which is sufficient of itself to remove all doubt in the popular mind as to their connection with the Evil One. In spite, however, of this disreputable association, kinship with a witch gives one a certain social status, and an old gamekeeper of our acquaintance undoubtedly derives much of his credit as a local oracle from the circumstance that his mother was a notorious witch. It is related of this woman, that one day, furious at seeing a coachman who was driving his master, a magistrate, to Quarter Sessions, whip round at her boys who were running behind the carriage, she warned him that "he'd remember that" the next time he came that way. Accordingly, when on the return journey they had reached this self-same spot, the wheels locked, and the carriage suddenly stopped. Not all the efforts of the horses, who tugged till they were white with lather, could move it one inch. The blacksmith was sent for, but he could not make the wheels go round, "and that didn't move till the sun set, and as soon as ever as that was set, off it went, quite easy, of itself."

It is a little strange that not even the shadow of a tradition remains of the burning of witches; and in place of ducking we have simpler tests and remedies, in many of which pins play a prominent part, probably only because a pin is the most handy of domestic implements. Thus, should you be desirous of finding out whether So-and-so is a witch, watch her as she comes along, and when she has passed, stick a pin into the track left by the heel of her boot. Then, await her return. Should she be a real witch, she will never come back that way. Should she even get as far as the pin, she cannot pass it; she must turn round, and go some other way.

Or, again. Mrs. Davis had a beautiful brood of strong healthy chicks. Each morning as she was feeding them one would suddenly fall over on its back and die. She had lost several in this mysterious way, when one morning, just as a chick was in the act of tumbling over, she snatched it up, and took its liver out. This she carried indoors, and, sticking a pin through it, set it up on the mantelshelf. Then she told the boys to watch, and tell her if they should see Mother Pocock coming that way. Presently, "'Mother,' they says, 'here she comes!'" She came along till she got to the bottom of the lane, and then she stopped, and turned back. She could not come any further, and she never came that way again, nor did any more of the chickens die.

Another remedy consists in burning a bottle containing portions of the victim. For instance, the following story is gravely told :—" Farmer So-and-so's daughter was terrified uncommon by old Dame White. She couldn't get no peace nohow. So he goes to the cunning man, and *he* tells him what to do. Says he, 'You get a little bottle, put some water, some pins, and some of her hair in it, and then set it in the fire, and watch that till it's burnt. Mind you close up every chink, crack, and keyhole, and don't you say nothing to nobody while that's agoing on.' Well, he did as he was bid to, and closed up every chink, as he thought, and put the bottle in the fire. And all the time that that was a-burning this 'ere old Mother White she kept on a-running round the house screaming and trying to get in. At last she did find a crack somewhere, and came in like a little spannel dog, and set her fore feet up on the hearth, and then *that* wasn't no good."

"Cunning men" are sometimes very useful. Should you lose anything, and fancy it is stolen, the cunning man will make an image of the article appear on the face of the thief.

Belief in the mysterious shows itself in many startling stories. One woman, when a girl at school, picks up a bag of feathers which she finds in a wood. As she carries it away it gets heavier and heavier, until she can no longer mount the hill. So she turns, and, with exceeding difficulty, begins to carry it back. And now the bag gets lighter and lighter, until at last she restores it to its original position with its gravity unchanged. As she tells the story now, many big, strong boys were unable to lift the bag from the ground; but, this deducted, we may remember that she was a child then, and conscience is a potent witch. Another woman, after letting in, as she supposes, her drunken master on a dark night, turns round, to find, not her master, but a big black dog. She gives it a kick, and, to use her own words, "that goes up like a bunch of feathers!"

Just below the church lies a moated manor-house fronted with a beautiful Tudor keep. Once the home of two ill-fated Queens of England, it has now, sad to say, long been used only as a farmhouse. In the thirties of the present century the tenant of the time, riding home one night from market, was set upon and shot. The murder was not brought home to any one, though a farmer who was married out of hand by the dead man's widow was commonly believed to have been guilty of the crime. So far the facts. Now for the sequel, as told to me by an old woman, living still. She assured me it was matter of common knowledge when she was a girl, and that she had heard her father, a farmer of some standing, speak of it himself. We will have it—with a change of names—in her own words.

"Well, do you blef thisyer Nat Bramber could rest? He couldn't. He wur always bad, though some times he wur wurser nor some. He would come back whiles at night, and be that troubled to get in at the castle geate. 'I *will* come in—I *will* come in' the men used to hear him saying. That was thisyer dead un withstood him. At last there was no bearing with it ; thisyer ghost was for to be laid. So the ministers came from all round, and each brought a candle. In the middle of the big hall was set a basin, and that was filled with Red Sea water. And they each said his prayers for to lay this dead un's ghost. And first one's candle went out and then another's, and then *he* was bet. At last none of 'em couldn't go on, 'cept Muster Cowley. That's faather of *old* Muster Cowley "—alluding to an old clergyman since dead. "He kep on, though his candle was getting lower and lower. At last, just when that was a-going right out, thisyer dead un was druv into the water. He didn't want to't ; he was druv. ' And mussy,' I've heard my faather say, ' didn't that ere steam and fizzle ! ' "

Superstition dies hard. And, if it should seem strange to some that, though living in the country, they have never heard of these things as a matter of present belief, they must remember that the poor are extremely sensitive and reticent on any points about which they feel they are likely to be laughed at. They will tell you nothing till they know you well, and, if directly challenged, next to nothing then.

OXFORD: THE UPPER RIVER

OXFORD: THE UPPER RIVER

Oxford, like Central Africa, has a strange fascination over her sons. Like Central Africa, too, she offers a boundless field to observation and research. A many-sided man may live in Oxford half a dozen different lives, and keep them all distinct. But the typical man, asked for his most pleasant recollection of Oxford life, would probably reply, if he belonged to the later development, "footer," or "socker," or "togger" (names he would trace to obsolete derivations), or, if he were a wag, "the proggins." One can imagine the howl of contempt which would greet such an answer as "the upper river." The "smug's" river. What, by the way, exactly is a smug? Men belonging to other colleges would possibly suggest "a —— man." But that, of course, is no definition.

Yet the upper river has a charm that is all its own. The lower river is a training course; it flows below and away from the town, and drains it of boating men from every quarter. Men go on the lower river for business purposes, and not to look about; and this is just as well, as for a long way below beautiful Iffley there is little to be seen. Even spires and towers have disappeared, so high are the banks on either side. Nuneham is very pretty, no doubt, but with a prettiness of the tea-tray order—that is to say, Nature here is prim and over-aided. Nuneham is always quite tidy and in her company manners, she requires red parasols and bright dresses, and without them she is incomplete.

One natural feature of interest there is indeed at Nuneham. This is a pool sacred to the water-soldier. Not a Royal Marine, but a plant* which you will not find growing everywhere. This plant resembles in general appearance the top of a pine-apple. During the greater part of the year it lives under water, burying its roots in the mud. But under a summer impulse it weighs its anchors one by one, and, rising to the surface, courts the sun. And now it sends out many suckers, which bear young plants at their extremities like the young plants of the strawberry. Each of these gives rise to a stalk, from the middle of its whorl of

* *Stratiotes aloides.*

leaves, which in due time bears a fair white flower. The seed is ripened under water, for, their flowering over, the plants, now grown mature, descend to their muddy bed.

The upper river stops short of the town. Pure and clean it comes, from its rising at Thames Head away up in the Gloucester hills, past Tadpole Weir, and a dozen other points of interest, to New Bridge, where the Windrush has carved itself a sparkling mill pool as it comes in from Witney Town. And so the river runs on to beautiful Bablock Hythe, where is one of the few remaining ferry-boats built large enough to take over a team of horses, their waggon, and its load of hay. At Pinkhill Weir, just below, is another, a broader and truly magnificent pool. Many a noble trout has been taken out of "Pingle" Pool, and many a phantom minnow has been lost in its curling eddies, for there are treacherous logs and moss-covered boulders lying hidden there in places. When the floods are out in winter over the broad flat meadows, the ducks come there in some numbers; and the old lock-keeper will tell you the story of how he once stalked five wild swans. And now past Eynsham the river runs—Eynsham, which can boast the most beautiful bridge, Shillingford's excepted, on all the upper Thames. Old Dick Treadwell (pronounced Treddle), the tollgate-keeper, is worth a visit in himself. He is an enthusiast on the fiddle, as his father was before him; he remembers how his father once took him into Oxford to hear the "head fiddler that ever lived," and how his father told him that this wonderful performer got as much as "two pun a night!" Ah, you may wonder, but his father told him, so he knows it must be right. A curious camp-like prominence looks down upon the bridge, and round the shoulder of the hill lie the great woods that stretch away to Witham without a break. On the left the meadows widen back, and Cassington spire and Yarnton tower stand out sharp in the sunlight. Presently a turn of the stream brings distant Oxford into view. But Oxford is five miles further yet, and the river has many a long reach to pass, and an island where the otters eat their dinner, a bed of flowering-rush where the swans nest, King's Weir, and Godstow Abbey, and more long reaches before it comes to Medley Lock and ends as the upper river.

This, then, is a bird's-eye view of the upper river. It is early yet; we will take a dingey at Bossom's and spend a day up stream. Before evening ("Vincent's" derision notwithstanding) you shall surely be convinced that the smugs have the best of it.

There, we are not going to pull against time. You may light your pipe and lie back in the stern of the boat, and I will paddle you up stream and talk to you about the upper river.

How far shall we get? One cannot tell. It will depend entirely upon what there is to see and hear.

Close under the tow-path the stream is running swift and strong. But in only a narrow channel, for clean across to the other bank the river is one big shallow. Everywhere you may see the sunlight playing on the golden gravel. Myriads of tiny fish—fry, minnow, and bleak ("bly" in the language of Thames-side)—are darting about in shoals. Nature creates them in their millions because they have so many enemies. They carry their life—these little fish—in their fins, so to speak. Life would be unendurable could they anticipate; but I think they are always taken unawares. Now a thing that they took for a mussel-shell starts up, opens, and sinks again into the mud, and two or three of their number are missing—for an eel had been lying with his evil head just clear of the mud. Now a rainbow-coloured thing, flashing like Excalibur, comes headlong in from another world, and a kingfisher has carried off a gudgeon. And then all of a sudden, with a rush and a dash, a great spiny perch comes charging along, scattering the shoal in all directions, and when it closes up again there is a further gap in its numbers. There are many other enemies, and one that comes from far. When the common terns are moving overland on their way to nest by other waters, and when they are going back again, one or two will stay behind and fly sometimes for a couple of days together up and down this favourite reach. Very lovely they look, these white sea-swallows, and just a little strange, like angels "visiting the green earth"; they seem to bring a sound of far-off breakers, and it is hard at first to recollect that this is big Port Meadow, and we but half a mile from Medley Lock.

Have you ever seen tame geese fly? Not more than a few yards at a time, perhaps. Well, then, these Port Meadow geese can fly almost the whole length of the meadow without once touching ground. You may see them do it almost any evening. Use has kept their muscles trim. Darwin has told us how the vultures flock to their prey from amazing heights, each taking his cue from the next

.n order. And just so, when the cottagers open their back garden gates to feed the geese in the evening, the news spreads as if by magic, each little party hurrying up to its supper; those nearer running with outstretched wings, those down in the meadow—not to be forestalled—rising clear of the ground and flying right away to the top. They seldom get up higher than four feet, partly because they have no time to waste upon trajectories, and partly so that if their wings *should* give out they will not have far to fall.

Here the shallow suddenly deepens, and opposite these willows is the hole known as Black Jack. Ask a waterman about Black Jack, and he instantly becomes mysterious; he predicts that "we shall never know all that there is down there," and "reckons there are some things down there it's a good thing we can't see. Don't you, Bill?" And Bill confirms the suspicion. Tradition says that Black Jack is fathomless, and so it is—by sculls and boat-hooks.

The sandpipers are not here to-day, they are away nesting by the Gloucester streams; very soon they will be back with their young, and hunting for shrimps along low-water mark. As you approach they will circle out over the stream with plaintive piping, to settle a few yards further on—a manœuvre they repeat a dozen times. Their place is taken now by the yellow wagtail, whose tactics are much the same. As beautiful as a humming-bird is Ray's wagtail, and almost as quick upon the wing. They are the constant companions of the Port Meadow cattle, attracted by the swarms of insects that come where cattle feed.

Let us fasten the painter to this little bridge and explore for a few yards this tiny stream. We have not time to examine it minutely, but must just notice these two plants. They are not rare, but are worth noticing because, like the water-soldier, they are local plants. Among the primulas is one genus which includes two species only. One is a North American, the other an English plant. Here it is—*Hottonia*, the water-violet, and is flowering very late this year. The other we shall not find so easily. There, you see that hairy-looking weed floating about in thick bunches. It is *Utricularia*, the bladderwort, in some respects one of the most interesting of all our British plants. Not because of its flowers, which are yellow and ordinary, but because of a curious habit. It is a carnivorous plant. The little bladders interspersed among the leaves are each provided with a trap-door. Should any prying larva or inquisitive little fry look in at the door in passing, his fate is sealed. He is caught, and drawn into a chamber of death from which there is no escape. A plant if kept in an aquarium will soon catch in this way most of the small things about—for instance, tiny fish, the larvæ of gnats, and even *Daphnia*, in spite of his shell. *Drosera*, the sundew, drains the insects of their juices as soon as they are caught. The bladderwort, on the contrary, simply holds its prisoners captive till they die, and then, it is said, feeds on the products of decay.

Now we must get back to our boat.

Look at that gaunt grey sentinel watching us from over the meadow. There are always a few herons' nests in Witham Woods, and this bird has come from there. He is waiting for frogs, and perhaps for a water-rat. As soon as we are safe away he will turn to his task again: lowering his head, rounding his shoulders, and watching on. Here we have reached the first ford (as far as I know) on the Thames. A man can walk across here in summer without getting wet above his knees. The ford is white with beds of water-crowfoot—a common flower, but, like many common flowers, with its own special interest. Nature has adapted it remarkably to the conditions of its life. It has two distinct forms of leaves. On the top of the water it bears stout, flat, ovate leaves, which serve the double purpose of buoying it up and of presenting a wide surface to the action of the air and sun; but those which are swaying in the current underneath are modified to simple bunches of hair-like filaments. Over these the current has little power, since they yield to every impulse of the stream.

And here at last is Godstow Abbey, beautiful even now in its decay. Not so very long ago, when the navvies were making the new cut to let the floods off, they dug up some stone coffins and many mouldering bones; and before authority had time to intervene, hese bones were hawked about for sale by the loafers of the bridge. Were some of those Fair Rosamond's? I cannot tell; but the old chroniclers have it that she was laid to rest at first within the chapel walls, till, in obedience to Hugh of Lincoln's stern command, the remains were removed elsewhere—perhaps just outside the walls. But, wherever the place, we may be sure the good nuns laid her lovingly, for until that fatal day when her peace of mind was broken by the glitter of a Court, she had been ever welcome within the abbey walls, where all were the brighter for her fairness and her wit.

OXFORD: THE UPPER RIVER

And now here is something that seems more vividly even than the grey walls themselves to put us in touch with that old time. These good nuns were no cloistered mystics—they were the ministers to the poor for miles around. And do you see this curious plant growing under the wall, with the heart-shaped leaf and the yellow trumpet flower? It is not a native of England, but was planted here by the nuns. Why? Because it is *Aristolochia*, the birthwort, and was useful as a medicine in certain cases, as its name implies.

What a little way we have come! and there is ever so much more to see and hear. It is getting so late that all we can do now is to leave the boat and hurriedly walk to King's Weir. You will seldom see finer silver poplars than those that grow in Godstow Wood. Do you notice how the trees are riddled by the goat-moth caterpillar? This is a favourite wood, too, for lime and poplar hawks and other *Sphingidæ*. Had we time we could easily find a nightingale's nest. There are always one or two in this wood, and the sedge-warblers nest here in numbers. The reed-warbler also makes its lovely pendant nest in the reeds that flank the edge. In the matted roots of that fallen poplar which we can just see from here a pair of kingfishers have nested for many years. The boys cannot reach the nest because of the deep pool of water which the torn-up roots have left. And hobbies breed here every year. Fortunately for themselves, they do not come to this country until the leaf is on the trees. Sometimes they nest in an old kestrel's nest, and sometimes in that of a crow. They have a pretty habit of toying about just over the tops of the trees like large moths. Even an inexperienced hand may know them by their white throats. They live almost entirely on insect life, though the keepers will not credit this.

All those holes in the bank are made by the crayfish. The Thames-side loafers catch them in a flat muslin net baited with bits of meat.

We must particularly notice this still backwater, not only because of the beautiful lily-like *Limnanthemum* (it has, I think, no English name) and *Ranunculus lingua*, the noble water-spearwort, but because it is the home of one of the most fascinating creatures in all the range of animal life—namely, *Argyronetron*, the water-spider—the first who made the diving-bell. Watch it at its work. First of all it makes the bell: weaving it round and round, closer and closer, till the web is air-tight all throughout; then it lashes it firmly to the neighbouring plants, and so begins to fill it. Now comes the most wonderful part. Swimming to the surface of the water, it turns tail upwards, and with its two hindermost legs takes literally a piece of air, which it carries as a bubble down below. Conveying the bubble to the mouth of the bell, it lets it go. The bubble floats up inside the bell, and the first movement is complete. It only remains to do this again and again, until gradually the bell is full of air, and hangs there as large as a silver thimble, and as bright as a ball of mercury.

And here is King's Weir, and there is a large trout on the rise. You may put any common brown trout into the Thames, and soon they shall be as big as this. The Thames men say it is from feeding on the bly.

There, now, we must be getting back to Medley Lock. Medley itself belonged to the abbey; it was given to the nuns by Robert of Witham. The old writers say it was the "middle-way"—that is, between Godstow and Oxford; and that it was a place of great resort for " divers pleasures."

Now you have seen a little of the upper river by day, but you must not think you know it yet. When you have seen it in the dawn—when you have felt your way at night, round every winding reach, and listened to and learnt the meaning of some of the night-voices—then, and not till then, may you fairly claim to know a little of the upper river. Yes, here are the verses. It is early morning. Listen.

KING'S WEIR.

Hung in the hand of dawn a few
    Chill stars are paling to their death
Above the meadows white with dew,
    And heavy with the orchis' breath.

Where bees protest a drowsy tale,
    And plaintive peewits fall and twist,
And in the mowing-grass the rail—
    A strident-voiced ventriloquist—

Creeps between challenging and fear,
    And the small bat eccentric flits—
Taking the moth—and on the Weir
    A single yellow-wagtail sits.

And, wakened by the wakening morn,
    The herald breeze begins to blow,
But now a doubtful murmur born
    Of shivering hill-side beach, and now

It makes the silver poplars gleam,
    And fans the thistles into play,
And whitens all the stiller stream,
    And passing sighs itself away.

But it has left the water glad,
    And made the big trout plunge and hurl
His length into the foam, and add
    A breaking circle to the swirl.

And now down all the roads of dawn
    Comes in the tide of gold, the same
That lights the diamond on the lawn,
    Or rages till the prairies flame.

I see it draw the wreathèd woof
    Of veiling mist across the plain;
I see it glinting on the roof
    And burning on the burnished vane;

Lighting the sedge-bird's secret place,
    Lifting the windflower's tired head,
Blushing upon the briar's face
    And laughing in the iris-bed;

And the great soul of earth, that moves
　　In all I see or cannot see,
Springs, radiant at the touch it loves,
　　A nameless ecstasy.

UPON A DAY

UPON A DAY

THE tent is pitched some ten feet above the river, just in the point that is made by the meeting of the river and the brook. The river here forms a horseshoe, and from the tent door you have a clear view down either curve. A lock connects the two heels of the horseshoe, so there is no traffic past the tent. It is impossible, indeed, to pass up this way into the river above, because of a tumbling bay.

Our little promontory is the extremest point of a meadow that is quite remarkable in itself. It is full of grand old trees; sycamore, chestnut, oak, and lime —none more noble than two mighty elms that rear themselves up high into the sky, and widen out below into a rugged platform, on which several persons may sit. Further on are three magnificent cedars of Lebanon, whose arms stretch right across the brook. They belong not of right to an English scene. They were planted long ago, perhaps to commemorate a royal visit. For this was then the inclosure of a religious house. But little of the abbey is remaining now. You may trace the foundations here and there, and in the farmhouse across the meadow are one or two old mullioned windows that have evidently seen better days, and that is all. I should have said that the whole of the space included in the horseshoe is filled by a large osier-bed—a roddam, as it is called on the Thames. But the willows are so wide apart that there is plenty of room for a jungle-growth of nettles, comfrey, and giant water-docks.

Such, then, are, roughly speaking, the surroundings of the tent. Men in houses, where wooden shutters and close-drawn blinds shut out the day, sleep heavily and late. But here, though sleep is sound, there is no slow returning to consciousness. Lightly plays the breath of morn with the loose canvas of the tent-door, and as lightly the sleeper awakes from sleep. He was asleep, he is awake; and that is all. At once alert, conscious, himself, he is looking out upon the infancy of a new-born summer day.

It is an enchanting scene. The sky (how far away it seems!) is some cold, clear tint of palest green, more subtle than any painter ever put on canvas yet. In the south a single star is twinkling to the dawn.

High up among the fleecy clouds the young moon rides—a silver gondola. Low in the east, just topping a line of elms, stretches a long black cloud, shaped like some dragon of the prime. Glassily smooth flows the river, excepting where the breeze has caught it, and turned it into silver light.

And this tent-dweller has nothing to do all day. Think what it means. A whole long day to be idle in! Never mind the grammar. Grammar was made for those who have to work: for there are persons who are obliged to work. There are some poor things, who, even on this very day, and when the sun is at its hottest, and Throgmorton Street is for all the world like the furnace-rooms of Woolwich Arsenal, will be swarming like blackbeetles out of all the cracks in that stone-built oven, happy in the knowledge, or delusion, that they see their way to gold.

But our tent-dweller has little time to spare for thoughts on such sad themes. In a very few minutes now dawn—the half-light—will be over: day—the sunlight—will be here. It lasts, this border-time, but some brief half-hour; but that half-hour is full of interest, for it closes in the little hidden dramas of the night. The tent-dweller is setting out; let us go too. We must not go *with* him, because we should see nothing then. Nature, believe me, is not so easily seen. To all the blackbeetle Throgmorton Street swarms she rolls herself up like a hedgehog. They repel her as "with a pitchfork." "Gently, and one at a time," is her motto. So we cannot go with the tent-dweller; but still, you shall not lose, for I will be your *Diable boiteux* and show you what he sees, and how he manages to see it.

See his dress. How carefully its colour is chosen! It is hard, indeed, to say what its colour is. It is neither drab, nor grey, nor green, but something perhaps of each of these. It is indefinite, but it harmonises so cleverly with any surroundings that it needs a quick eye to detect the wearer at the distance even of a hundred yards. The tent-dweller knows that the first principles for the study of all wild animals, from tigers to water-rats, are three in number, and are these—

Keep out of their sight.

Keep out of their hearing.

Keep out of their field of smell.

Wild creatures have an instinctive dread of anything white. You cannot stop out your rabbits more effectually, if the days and nights are quiet, than by the simple plan of placing pieces of white paper in the mouth of their holes; an envelope fixed into a split stick and stuck up at the end of the hedge will keep the cock pheasants in, and spare the need of human stops, as every keeper knows.

The hearing of wild creatures is marvellously acute; and, of all possible noises, nothing alarms them half so much as the sound of the human voice. This particular sound travels a long way, and the wild animal with its ear close to the ground has timely warning of any coming danger. It is no exaggeration to say that the voice of ordinary conversation will put on the *qui vive* any creature within a radius of a quarter of a mile, and much further even than this in hilly districts. We have all seen, at some time or other, an elderly sportsman's gesticulations as he inveighs in early English against the wildness of the "beastly birds," quite blind to the fact that his own voice has long ago put up the heads of every partridge on the place.

Whether the sense of smell of birds is as acute as that of mammals is a disputed point. There are good grounds for supposing that it is comparatively but little developed; and that the decoy-man who carries a bit of burning turf when he visits his decoys is the victim of a baseless superstition.

But to return to the tent-dweller, who has suddenly stopped as if frozen into stone. He is only looking at a water-rat, but yet the common water-rat—or, more properly, the water-vole—regarded from what point you please, is well worthy of study. It is one of our most interesting English animals. It is not very easy to point to any great structural differences between it and the rat. Those grinding teeth have no roots; and, for the rest, the distinctions are chiefly superficial, and these you may notice for yourself. Its head is broader and shorter than that of the rat; its tail is shorter, blunt, and covered with hair. Its ears are also hairy, and not naked as the rat's. But it is in habit that the great difference lies. The barn-rat can swim well, but he is a land-lubber in comparison with his aquatic cousin. The barn-rat is omnivorous, as the housekeeper knows to her cost; the water-rat is almost entirely a vegetable feeder. Not entirely, for at certain seasons of the year he too acquires a taste for meat; but this is not his rule. Look at the little creature. It is still, and almost of the same colour as the alder stub on which it sits. It knows this, and it is so still, not, you may be sure, because it does not see the tent-dweller, but because it trusts it is itself unseen. But the watcher stands there also motionless, and it soon forgets its fears, and begins to prepare for breakfast. Slipping silently into the water, it makes for a little patch of reeds. Suddenly it dives, and one of the reeds begins to quiver. A skilful woodman is at work below. Presently the reed floats out flat on the top of the water, cut off cleverly close to the root. Often the diver will reappear at once; but sometimes it will cut two or three reeds consecutively, and then coming to the top seize first one and then the others by the white succulent end, and swim off with them to its seat. When it has a great burden, or is in a hurry—and it is always in a hurry for breakfast—it swims with all its feet. At other times it uses its hind feet only, carrying its fore-limbs at its side as the harbour seals their flippers.

But see the tent-dweller. By that quick turn of his head you may know that something has arrested his attention, and he seems to be listening intently. Stay. Do you hear that curious whistling sound coming from the reed-bed beyond the cedars? It is an otter coming home from his travels of the night. To the tent-dweller the sound is familiar as that of a human voice. Off he sets at top speed, and does not stop till he has reached the nearest cedar. Leaning there, almost hidden by the trunk, he knows he is safe from discovery, for the breeze is blowing in his face. Nearer and nearer comes the whistling sound, and then for a minute all is still. Presently round a corner of the stream comes, not the otter, to all appearance, but a wave; the otter is swimming under the water. But now he is out upon a shallow, a beautiful picture of activity and strength. In his flat head, his powerful jaw, and his muscular shoulder there is expressed, not cunning so much, perhaps, as precision and secrecy. If I wanted an agent to do me some dark deed, I would choose, not the fox, I think, but the otter. He would travel like a very power of darkness, swiftly, secretly, and strike as surely as the vendetta, not one single second too early or too late. When he is on the hunt he has no need to chase the fish; he can scent them, even from the bank, and, slipping into the water without a sound, is upon them before they are aware. And our otter now has slipped into the water, and is coming quickly down stream, but with no more sound than if he were swimming in oil. He emerges directly under the roots of the third cedar; a moment's pause, and in a single bound he is up among the roots and out of sight. And now, if you look closely, you may see a large dark hole, well guarded by the twisted roots of this old tree. Oh yes, the tent-dweller knew it long ago, and has been on the look-out ever since he first noticed the otter's seal or footprint in the mud. But he has had long to wait, for otters are great travellers, and one has not been here for days. Why do not the hounds come here and hunt? Because it is too near to the big river, and once there the otter could laugh at his foes.

Now there flies past a beetle, larger than a dor-beetle, but flying with less noise. Suddenly it drops head foremost into the water; not into the brook, indeed, but into a stagnant ditch that opens out of it. It is *Dyticus*, the great water-beetle, and this is its curious habit. It is aquatic all the day, aërial all the night. I do not find that any one has tried to explain this strange contradiction. By all the laws of residential life the water is his home. In the water lie all his seeming interests, his food, his loves, his foes. He was hatched under the leaf of the water-lily, and there, or thereabouts, he passed from a long-bodied hungry larva to a hunched-back helpless chrysalis; and, by-and-by, with torpedo-like body and swimming legs, broke loose, a perfect water-beetle. How, then, can we account for this irregular habit? Is it not just possible that it may be connected with the process of respiration? The water-beetle is a strong-swimming creature, and needs a large amount of air for oxidation of its blood. The beetles possess, in connection with their tracheal system, a series of air-cells analogous to the air-spaces of birds; until these are filled they are unable to rise, and they are filled by the motion of the wings. May it not be that *Dyticus* retains this collected air in these tracheal dilatations, as in reservoirs, as residual food for his tissues during the day?

What hoarse, ill-omened scream was that? It is as if some old chiding witch were passing on her broomstick through the trees.

A white owl is going back to its hollow in the sycamore. How dreamily soft is its flight! The whooping of a pigeon's or a peewit's wings would be plainly heard at that distance. But this bird sails noiselessly and soft, as down or feathers wafted on space. He is one of the few owls that call habitually when on the wing. His cousin, the tawny owl, for example, rarely utters his beautiful hoot excepting when at rest. Do you notice that this bird is carrying something in its talons? One cannot see at this distance what it is, but the tent-dweller could tell us it is a field-mouse, and that it is the last of many that the bird has been carrying to its young ones every few minutes through the night.

In the sycamore now the babies are snoring, as you may hear them at sermon-time in a country church. For this is the owl of church towers and hollow trees, while the tawny, like the long-eared owl, oftener nests in places quite exposed.

But the east is beginning to redden now. Dark, almost to blackness, stands out our line of elms, clear-cut against a band of crystal sky, that slowly widens with the rising of the curtain of the night. And now long, rose-coloured filaments begin to feel their way up through the diaphanous haze of the lower zones, and now the warm glow catching, slowly at first, leaps from cloud to cloud, till the whole wide eastern sky is ablush like the peach-gardens of the south. But the elms and the broad meadows round them are not lighted yet. Now turn round and see how great the difference; for

—not by eastern windows only,
When daylight dawns, comes in the light,
In front the sun climbs slow, how slowly,
But westward, look, the land is bright.

Before he lights the fire for breakfast our friend will have his morning swim. It is less a swim than an exploration. Instead of amusing himself by taking noisy headers, he slips quietly into the water from the stern of his boat, and with a few strokes, just to stretch his limbs, sinks till there is little else but his eyes above the water, and drops down stream. It is an old ruse, and one which the West Indians practise with a view to catching water-fowl. The hunter fits over his head a calabash, and, surrounded by empty, floating gourds, is borne right into the midst of the unsuspecting wildfowl. Gourds or no, this is the way to study the habits of those birds that live where water runs. And now a pair of swans are bringing their brood of five up from the lower reaches, where they have been all night. Stately and slow they come, the male bird leading, and the young strung out in a line behind him. The female brings up the rear. Quaint little things are the soft grey cygnets, and when they come to a bit of rapid water, it is funny to see them all turn at exactly the same angle, so as to neutralise the pressure of the stream; taking it slantingly, as a brewer's horse takes the hill.

The sand-martins have drilled their tunnels into the bank, where it is, from turf to water, not more than five feet high. It is an impossibility for even the most practised swimmer to remain absolutely motionless in fresh water for more than a few moments at a time.

But the sand-martins take no notice of the swimmer's head. In and out of their nests they dart, twittering cheerily all the while. Poor little birds! They have chosen a risky nesting-place. Sometimes there comes a summer flood, and then all their nursery cares are gone for nothing. It is true they may make a second nest, but it surely must be weary work, unattended though it seems to be with any sense of loss of interest.

Even the sharp eye of the kingfisher is deceived at first. From his perch on a dead alder-bough he flashes like a jewel into the stream, sending up a little cloud of spray, as with a single movement he seizes a minnow and returns to his vantage point. It is only in the early morning that the kingfisher fishes here: at other times of the day he is in seclusion up the brook. Very beautiful is the brook in itself and in all its surroundings. Every river feature is to be found here in little. Here it flows in deep, dark pools where the big white-lipped chub lie wary and expectant, waiting for moth or caterpillar to drop from off the soft blue willows that almost span the stream. Here it tinkles fairy music over tiny waterfalls, and on again past brown stones and golden gravel to where broad beds of flowering crowfoot show up like snow in the noonday sun. The very banks themselves are beautiful; not only for the jewelling of the honey-suckle or the pink dog-rose, but because of the common nettle, water-dock, meadow-sweet, and yellow ragwort that help to give the brook its own identity, closing it in and screening it from the rude gaze of things outside.

In one spot only is the luxuriance of plant life less than tropical, and here there is none at all. This spot is under the cedars. There is a solitude of majesty, and no plants may flourish there. Only the rabbits burrow round about, and the otter finds a home beneath their overhanging roots. Close to them is the tent-dweller's favourite post, and here he will lie, sometimes for hours, in the hottest part of the day. Idling? Well, yes, I suppose it is idling; at least, that is what Throgmorton Street would say. He is so still you might suppose him fast asleep. But, in truth, every sense is strung to its highest pitch. Nothing escapes him. Not the briefest shadow of a passing bird: not the faintest rustle in the grass. He can see and learn more in this way in a single hour than if he were to walk a whole day up the brook. That is the way to study Nature. Go a hundred yards away from the house in any direction, and be still. Wild things are all about you then. The way through the wood, that now seems so deserted, was an animated scene just before you came along. It is your voice, your tread, your shadow, and (forgive me, dear reader) your smell, that have wrought the change; even though, as is most improbable, the jays did not see you, and scream danger ahead. But, back to the cedars.

Lie down with the tent-dweller flat on the ground, and look steadily into this deep, dark pool—deep, that is, relatively. It seems at first to be quite empty—quite fathomless. But soon the bottom grows distinct, and certain little rays of light are seen glancing on stones and roots, and water-grass that moves in waving tresses. And presently a creature, scarlet and blue, and of any and every tint between these two, as the light takes it, comes into view. It is a male stickleback. He is keeping guard over his nest—that small, irregular bunch of weed, in the middle of which his partner and her eggs are hidden. It is only at this season that he is gorgeous in his suit of scintillating armour. And so he keeps his watch—a perfect Paladin—and so he holds the field against all comers, secure in his suit of armour and his bristling spines. And then, with a sound of rushing wind, a wood-pigeon drops down to drink.

Of all the birds that haunt our woodlands, the pigeon is perhaps most wide awake. You will not easily catch him napping. He does not even drink like other birds. He does not sip and hold his head up to let the water trickle down his throat; he just takes <u>one</u> long steady pull, and then he is off again to the bean-field.

Time would fail to tell of all or of one-half of the incidents of humble life that come under the tent-dweller's ken in even this one sleepy hour of a broiling summer day; of the cock-pheasant, radiant in purple and gold, who comes down to drink, walking, delicately as Agag, through the nettles; of the caddis-worm, architect and builder, collecting sticks and shells for the castle he will bear about with him through life; of the caddis-flies, rising buoyant through the water, and, dry almost at once, stretching their wings to lose themselves forthwith in the quivering noonday heat. There is much indeed to see, but the tent-dweller notes it all. And could we stay, we too might come to see it with his eyes. But our holiday is all but over, and we have many a mile to go ere night.

May I drop the historic present—for all this happened long ago—and just tell you what the tent-dweller has himself said since of this same day? He said that on this day he did not find his way back to the tent until long after the dew had settled down upon the meadows, the summer moon had risen on the river, and the barn owl had set out anew in quest of mice; that he remembered this day especially well because of some lines which came to him while yet he lay awake. They were these:

> *Brook tinkling clear,*
> *The close defences of thy woven bowers*
> *Are sweet and spangled through. Here let me lie,*
> *And win thy secrets from the careless flowers,*
> *Who take them from thee all too easily.*
> *No wiles of love shall cheat my tongue; no fear,*
> *None—though the tidal sea itself should clamour here.*
>
> *Sing, ripple, sing—*
> *But I have seen thy brown and seething flood*
> *Rouse the big salmon out beyond the nets—*
> *A mile across the blue. And I have stood*
> *Where floodgates fail and death his pleasure gets.*
> *Though here—so kind thy court—the rudest thing*
> *Is the small tyrant minnow deftly skirmishing.*

And ere another verse could frame itself he was asleep.

THE PROCESSION OF SPRING

THE PROCESSION OF SPRING

IN the heart of a big city there lived a very learned botanist. *Campylotropous, quintuplinerved, tetradynamous*, not a flower of them all could puzzle him—he was a very learned botanist.

None the less there was a great blank in his life, and it was this. He had never seen the blue bird's-eye speedwell. Brown and dry, indeed, he kept within a book a thing that once had been that flower, and he could look at that. But *that* is not to see the bird's-eye speedwell.

The forget-me-not he had seen, for the forget-me-not is sold in penny bunches in the street. Not so the speedwell. Once plucked, the bloom falls off and floats down at your feet. The speedwell loves the bit of bank that bounds its home. It knows no other world, nor cares to know; and it is well—the lark knows where to find it when he drops from skies not bluer than itself.

The forget-me-not's is "the higher mission," you say? It may be so. But we were speaking not of missions, but of facts. And the fact remains that the speedwell never left the bank, and so the botanist had never seen the speedwell. For he had but one holiday in all the year, and that was at Christmas-time, when he went to see his old mother.

And as to missions: it is not given to every one to have "high missions," if that means going far afield. If Don Quixote had stayed at home, had looked after the old women and tried the poachers, the world would have been the loser, but perhaps he would have done more good in his day.

I fear that could our botanist have seen the speedwell on its bank he would have given it welcome only as *Veronica chamædrys*, an hypogynous, scrophularious, monopetalous dicotyledon. "His line," as he said, "was classification." So that, I suppose, was his mission. And no unworthy mission either. For a love of classification is a love of order, and that at least is a function of the Mind Supreme.

The speedwell has its mission all the same, but more of that by-and-by.

However firm the hold of winter on the land, even that strong hand must at last grow weary, and one by one slip out between its loosened fingers the laughing spirits born of spring.

The loveliest pearls that ever pleased a king are not more lovely than the bursting buds upon the willow. In significance, indeed, not half so beautiful. For the pearls that hold the yellow stamens in their folds are presageful of life, while the others are a product of disease.

Children love the budding willow. They call it "palm," and pick it as they come to school. But very soon they tire of its prettiness, and so the school-path is often strewn with willow. A royal freedom is this of childhood, that lays the whole round year under impost for its play. It is enough that the willow has ventured into the children's kingdom: childhood, imperious, claims it as of right.

Children, whose buoyant blood turns winter into summer, think not of catkins as a sign of spring. But suffering childhood and slow-moving age find here a dear delight. They have looked on so long and wistfully through the weary weeks of winter to where the sun is playing on the green and growing wheat. And so a little country child, with hip disease in a London hospital, cared little for all the hothouse flowers kind ladies brought her (she had so sweet a face), but lay always clasping tight a withered daffodil, and clasping it she died.

From the shallows of the pool over which the willow hangs there comes a voice of spring. It is the croak of frogs. There always seems something magical in the way the frogs appear in the pool. Yesterday not a frog was to be seen. There was the usual sprinkling of beetles, effets, and water-spiders, but not a single frog. This morning as soon as the sun began to warm the water the croaking began on all sides. The shallows are dotted with the brown heads of many frogs. Make the slightest movement, and instantly every head disappears. Presently from some corner the croaking begins again in a tentative, intermittent manner. It is not easy to detect the croaker, because at first he keeps himself carefully submerged, allowing only his nose and eyes to break the surface; reminding one of the pictures of the river-horse in books upon African travel. But presently, grown confident, he will raise his whole head, sending little ripples circling away with every beat of his white distended throat.

Frogs, I fancy, are fond of music. If on this first day of their arrival you sit quietly on the bank and whistle low and plaintively, they will all turn in your direction in apparent enjoyment. After a day or two the charm of music fails, for the frogs are busied in spawning.

When once the tadpoles are free they are beset with many foes. So that of all the myriad tadpoles hatched only a small number endure that change which is not the less wonderful because so familiar—the change from a vegetarian tadpole with gills and tail, to a tailless, air-breathing, insect-eating frog.

The sallow is the only bush now growing by the pool. Last year the underwood was cut, as it is cut every seventh year. No sooner is the sunlight so let in upon the pond than there comes up a thick growth of some aquatic mossy plant, clinging to stub and bottom. The dabchicks are very fond of the weed. They feed upon it and build their nests with it. These birds return with such regularity to these their haunts, that "have the dabchicks come?" becomes a standing question in the spring. The dabchicks may be there for days before you notice them. Very shy are they when first they come. So beware how you approach the pond. At the first glimpse of water, pause and glance carefully ahead, and you may chance to see the dabchick appear as if by magic on the surface of the pool. No diver ever dived for pearls so unweariedly as he for bits of weed. As he rises to the top he picks off the small crustaceans hidden in the leaves, snaps off the young shoot of the weed, and then he dives again. If at that instant you run forward at your best speed some dozen yards or so, and then again stay quiet as a stone, the bird on rising continues unsuspecting its pursuit. But move never so little, and like a flash it disappears, and, in a succession of rapid dives, soon is far away. There are divers and divers. The dabchick dives quite noiselessly, and that is the test of a true diver. By this you may know that it is accustomed to seek its food near the bottom and in deep water. Some birds dive chiefly for purposes of concealment and some for purposes of play. These last are clumsiest of all. Thus, the waterhen dives neatly but not noiselessly, the tame duck very clumsily and with much flapping of wings.

There surely never seemed so uncomfortable a nest as that of the dabchick. The guillemot who guards its single egg on the ledges of a wind-swept precipice is, one might suppose, cosily circumstanced by comparison. The nest itself is *in* not *on* the water, so that the dabchick almost sits in water as it sits upon its eggs. And whenever the bird leaves its nest it covers up its eggs with wet weed, and the eggs, white at first, soon become stained and brown. The nest is so deceptive in appearance—just a tangled mass of water-weed—that even the sharp eye of the schoolboy seldom finds it out.

For the direct opposite of this, see the nest of the waterhen. Fair and open, it is placed where the end of a sunken willow-bough peeps out of the water. The bird has just slipped off the nest. There are seven eggs already; it is easy enough to count them from the bank. The schoolboys found the nest some days ago. Next Saturday afternoon they will fish out all the eggs with a scoop at the end of a stick. A "goord" they call it; by which they mean a "goad." Poor moorhen! Her eggs make such a gallant show when threaded on a string.

Long before the moorhens began to build the rooks and jackdaws were hard at work. A pleasant scene is that of a rookery in early spring. Few sounds have so much power to recall forgotten scenes as the noise of building rooks. I think the caw of rooks would make an English Sunday in the middle of a desert. But grievous charges are brought against the rook, which, sad to say, cannot be disproved outright. The practice of shooting young rooks has been given up to a great extent of late years. So that rooks, it seems, are increasing in numbers, and northwards farmers have combined for their destruction. Well, a return to the rook rifle would soon thin their numbers to a sufficient extent. Let us have no murderous strychnine sown about the land. If rookeries must be destroyed wholesale, let it at least be those that are removed from dwellings, to save that stain on hospitality, the charge of confidence misplaced. For I have even known those that have ruthlessly destroyed this the chief ornament—a heronry excepted—of an ancient home.

But this is uncomfortable ground. It is pleasanter to think of those who would pour libations to the shade of Virgil if only rooks would come to their tall elms.

And if conditions are suitable they may be induced, by the following means, to come. Fasten up in the destined trees some half-score of imitation nests. To these bring nestlings from the nearest rookery. The old birds will find them out, feed them, rear them; and quite probably the next spring will see a rookery begun.

There are two plants of very different species which thrive exceedingly well under a rookery, and both are among the earliest flowers of spring. The first—dog-mercury—has a green-spiked flower; and the other, that forms a thick carpet of dark green heart-shaped leaves, has a flower that shines like a golden star, and is known to every one as the lesser celandine.

So, in spite of cruel winds of March, life is feeling its way on. Not these flowers alone, but coltsfoot, barren strawberry, daffodil, and primrose come into flower, and elder into leaf.

The tiny chiffchaff, our first bird of spring, hangs like a humming-bird on shivering wings, taking insects off the surface of the pool. The strange voice of the wryneck sounds about the orchard trees. The country folk call this the "snake-bird," because it scares the schoolboys by hissing like a snake when they approach its nest. The "cuckoo's mate" they call it too, though "cuckoo's messenger" would be the better name, for it always comes before the cuckoo.

The chirrup of the chiffchaff is cheery but monotonous, and goes to make more welcome the wild, bright song of the willow-wren, which comes in at the open windows a few mornings later on.

Both these birds build on the ground. Their nests are domed, and worked in, like the nests of field-mice, among the moss and grass of the pasture by the woodside. Both line their nests with feathers; but this the wood-wren, whose nest, externally, is so much like theirs, never does.

The wryneck, and all the tits, except of course the long-tailed tit, may easily be induced to nest in boxes fixed up in the garden trees. These tiny birds are marvellously bold when nesting. You may carry the box, nest, bird, and all from place to place, and provided you do so quietly the bird will not take wing.

About this time one begins to notice on the garden paths many tops of spruce-fir branches. The squirrel is the culprit. It is a pity he does this, as it prejudices the gardener against him. And why he does so it is hard to say, unless he has a taste for turpentine. The squirrel displays a great degree of cunning in the building, though none in the position, of its drey, or nest. Instead of springing from branch to branch as at other times, it runs with each load of moss or leaves to the base of the next tree, and so ascends. So that the drey is half finished before its presence is suspected. Yet, when surprised, the little creature holds its ground with a degree of boldness that would do credit to a lion. It will stamp and "chuckut," advancing and retreating in angry jerks as if daring us to attack. Like most nest-builders, it works hardest in the early morning. I am inclined to believe that the squirrel never moves at night. If this is so, it is the only strictly diurnal animal we possess.

Poor little red squirrel! I wonder when the day will come when its present persecutors, worthy cobnut persons in their way, shall have learnt to "be to his faults a little blind."

A warmer day than usual brings out the grass-snake. These reptiles are fond of entering the frames in which the gardener raises his seeds. They go there partly for warmth, and partly in search of frogs, which are attracted hither by the abundance of insect life. Later on the snake will lay its leathery eggs in the manure.

The country folk in certain parts are firmly persuaded that the adder as it grows old develops a pair of wings and flies about. They quite believe that they have seen it flying. This diabolical accomplishment intensifies the terrors of the "death-arder." Everything that creeps and looks like a snake is a death-adder. The idea arose in church, by mistake for "deaf adder," long years before the School Board came.

A glance at May, and we must bid farewell to the garden and the pool.

Very beautiful and bright are the children's garlands as they sing beneath the windows on the first of May:

> *This is the day, the first of May,*
> *Please to remember the garland day.*

So runs the couplet that exacts our pence. Remember it? No need to ask us that. The colonist at the other side of the world remembers it, and dreams of home. The convict as he picks his oakum remembers it, and is the better perhaps for the thought.

It is not only birds and children that May-day makes to sing. It beats a sort of song out of very humdrum lives—often but a clumsy rhythm, but perhaps a little gain on the workaday prose. I once knew a rhymer whose fancy it moved thus:

THE COMING OF SPRING.

An iron hand on a fettered land,
   Had faltered in grip at last,
And he settled low in his throne of snow,
   And his breath came hard and fast.

It powdered the mist upon rail and tree,
   It huddled the cows in the byre,
It buried the hares in a dusty drift,
   And scorched the young ash as fire.

THE PROCESSION OF SPRING

"They have cursed me long as the bringer of woes,
    The parent of fogs and sleets;
Did they know that I mellowed their land for the
    grain,
    And killed the disease in their streets?

"But a reign that had been more mild, itself
    Was ruled by a chance of birth,
When Æolus filled my lungs with breath
    So keen that it scathed the earth.

"You will lighten the touch of my iron hand,
    You will breathe where I would blow,
You will win more love from a thankless world
    Than Winter was born to know.

"Speed on, speed on," and he died in a blast
    That emptied the cells of the North;
And then, as a meteor from the bound
    Of heaven, the boy leapt forth.

He met on his way the whistling swans
    And the wild geese going home;
And laughed as he poised on his golden wings,
    For he knew that his strength was come.——

And sunshine flashed through the cold clear day
    And reddened the willow's shoot,
And put a love-note in the song of the lark,
    And a pulse in the violet's root.

He chanced on a child in a woodland path,
    All quiet and still in the sleep
That only the hungry and frozen know,
    And the boy was fain to weep.——

His tears fell hot on the ice-bound earth,
    And the mantle that Winter had spread
Ever grew less in the rain and the sun,
    And the corn lay green in its stead.

And things that had been in hiding long
    Crept out to the light of day:
The snake from the bank, the dreaming-mouse
    From chambered leaves and hay.

The mountain brook, unloosed once more,
    Went laughing to the flood,
And ferns hung nodding, damp and green,
    Where only boulders stood.

For, as dead embers fanned, the earth
   Grew bright beneath his wing,
Till a new world broke to a living flame,
   And sang to the light in Spring.

Yes, Spring had come. Spring with its story of hope. But even now Spring is yielding to a power fuller and higher yet, for greater than hope is assurance.

And from the grass of the bankside looks up a sky-blue flower, and seems to whisper, "Summer, dear Summer, is here."

That is the speedwell's mission.

VESPER

VESPER

The heron left her watch and hit the cloud,
   And laboured homewards to her wood of pines;
And, as the red west died, a wreathing shroud
   Came feeling on in weft of silver lines.
The laughter died out of the village street;
   The anvil's echoes sank into the hill;
The tower's challenging, low-tongued and sweet,
   A moment lingered—and the land was still.

So gently day his mantle round him drew,
   You had not known the moment he was hid,
But that the shy stars, shivering wan and few,
   Crept into place. And now the cricket chid
The chilling hours; and now the wanderer moon
   Moved into her blue sea with placid light,
And "Good-night" sighed the river's softened tune,
   And from the ether came again "Good-night."

Printed by BALLANTYNE, HANSON & CO.
London & Edinburgh.

MESSRS. LONGMANS, GREEN, & CO.'S
CLASSIFIED CATALOGUE

OF

WORKS IN GENERAL LITERATURE.

History, Politics, Polity, and Political Memoirs.

Abbott.—A HISTORY OF GREECE. By EVELYN ABBOTT, M.A., LL.D. Part I.—From the Earliest Times to the Ionian Revolt. Crown 8vo., 10s. 6d. Part II.—500-445 B.C. Cr. 8vo., 10s. 6d.

Acland and Ransome.—A HANDBOOK IN OUTLINE OF THE POLITICAL HISTORY OF ENGLAND TO 1890. Chronologically Arranged. By the Right Hon. A. H. DYKE ACLAND, M.P., and CYRIL RANSOME, M.A. Crown 8vo., 6s.

ANNUAL REGISTER (THE). A Review of Public Events at Home and Abroad, for the year 1892. 8vo., 18s.

> Volumes of the ANNUAL REGISTER for the years 1863-1891 can still be had. 18s. each.

Armstrong.—ELIZABETH FARNESE; The Termagant of Spain. By EDWARD ARMSTRONG, M.A., Fellow of Queen's College, Oxford. 8vo., 16s.

Arnold.—Works by T. ARNOLD, D.D., formerly Head Master of Rugby School.

> INTRODUCTORY LECTURES ON MODERN HISTORY. 8vo., 7s. 6d.
>
> MISCELLANEOUS WORKS. 8vo., 7s. 6d.

Bagwell.—IRELAND UNDER THE TUDORS. By RICHARD BAGWELL, LL.D. 3 vols. Vols. I. and II. From the first Invasion of the Northmen to the year 1578. 8vo., 32s. Vol. III. 1578-1603. 8vo., 18s.

Ball.—HISTORICAL REVIEW OF THE LEGISLATIVE SYSTEMS OPERATIVE IN IRELAND, from the Invasion of Henry the Second to the Union (1172-1800). By the Rt. Hon. J. T. BALL. 8vo., 6s.

Besant.—THE HISTORY OF LONDON. By WALTER BESANT. With 74 Illustrations. Crown 8vo. School Reading-book Edition, 1s. 9d.; Prize-book Edition, 2s. 6d.

Buckle.—HISTORY OF CIVILISATION IN ENGLAND AND FRANCE, SPAIN AND SCOTLAND. By HENRY THOMAS BUCKLE. 3 vols. Crown 8vo., 24s.

Chesney.—INDIAN POLITY: A View of the System of Administration in India. By Lieut.-General Sir GEORGE CHESNEY. New Edition, Revised and Enlarged.
[*In the Press.*

Crump.—A SHORT INQUIRY INTO THE FORMATION OF POLITICAL OPINION, from the reign of the Great Families to the advent of Democracy. By ARTHUR CRUMP. 8vo., 7s. 6d.

De Tocqueville.—DEMOCRACY IN AMERICA. By ALEXIS DE TOCQUEVILLE. 2 vols. Crown 8vo., 16s.

Fitzpatrick.—SECRET SERVICE UNDER PITT. By W. J. FITZPATRICK, F.S.A., Author of 'Correspondence of Daniel O'Connell'. 8vo., 7s. 6d.

Freeman.—THE HISTORICAL GEOGRAPHY OF EUROPE. By EDWARD A. FREEMAN, D.C.L., LL.D. With 65 Maps. 2 vols. 8vo., 31s. 6d.

History, Politics, Polity, and Political Memoirs—*continued.*

Froude.—Works by JAMES A. FROUDE, Regius Professor of Modern History in the University of Oxford.

THE HISTORY OF ENGLAND, from the Fall of Wolsey to the Defeat of the Spanish Armada.
Popular Edition. 12 vols. Crown 8vo., 3s. 6d. each.
Silver Library Edition. 12 vols. Crown 8vo., 3s. 6d. each.

THE DIVORCE OF CATHERINE OF ARAGON: the Story as told by the Imperial Ambassadors resident at the Court of Henry VIII. *In usum Laicorum.* Crown 8vo., 6s.

THE SPANISH STORY OF THE ARMADA, and other Essays, Historical and Descriptive. Crown 8vo., 6s.

THE ENGLISH IN IRELAND IN THE EIGHTEENTH CENTURY. 3 vols. Cr. 8vo., 18s.

SHORT STUDIES ON GREAT SUBJECTS. 4 vols. Cr. 8vo., 3s. 6d. each.

CÆSAR: a Sketch. Cr. 8vo., 3s. 6d.

Gardiner.—Works by SAMUEL RAWSON GARDINER, M.A., Hon. LL.D., Edinburgh, Fellow of Merton College, Oxford.

HISTORY OF ENGLAND, from the Accession of James I. to the Outbreak of the Civil War, 1603-1642. 10 vols. Crown 8vo., 6s. each.

A HISTORY OF THE GREAT CIVIL WAR, 1642-1649. 4 vols. Cr. 8vo., 6s. each.

THE STUDENT'S HISTORY OF ENGLAND. With 378 Illustrations. Cr. 8vo., 12s.

Also in Three Volumes.

Vol. I. B.C. 55—A.D. 1509. With 173 Illustrations. Crown 8vo. 4s.

Vol. II. 1509-1689. With 96 Illustrations. Crown 8vo. 4s.

Vol. III. 1689-1885. With 109 Illustrations. Crown 8vo. 4s.

Greville.—A JOURNAL OF THE REIGNS OF KING GEORGE IV., KING WILLIAM IV., AND QUEEN VICTORIA. By CHARLES C. F. GREVILLE, formerly Clerk of the Council. 8 vols. Crown 8vo., 6s. each.

Hart.—PRACTICAL ESSAYS IN AMERICAN GOVERNMENT. By ALBERT BUSHNELL HART, Ph.D., &c. Cr. 8vo., 6s.

Hearn.—THE GOVERNMENT OF ENGLAND: its Structure and its Development. By W. EDWARD HEARN. 8vo., 16s.

Historic Towns.—Edited by E. A. FREEMAN, D.C.L., and Rev. WILLIAM HUNT, M.A. With Maps and Plans. Crown 8vo., 3s. 6d. each.

BRISTOL. By the Rev. W. HUNT.
CARLISLE. By MANDELL CREIGHTON, D.D., Bishop of Peterborough.
CINQUE PORTS. By MONTAGU BURROWS.
COLCHESTER. By Rev. E. L. CUTTS.
EXETER. By E. A. FREEMAN.
LONDON. By Rev. W. J. LOFTIE.
OXFORD. By Rev. C. W. BOASE.
WINCHESTER. By Rev. G. W. KITCHIN, D.D.
YORK. By Rev. JAMES RAINE.
NEW YORK. By THEODORE ROOSEVELT
BOSTON (U.S.) By HENRY CABOT LODGE.

Horley.—SEFTON: A DESCRIPTIVE AND HISTORICAL ACCOUNT. Comprising the Collected Notes and Researches of the late Rev. ENGELBERT HORLEY, M.A., Rector 1871-1883. By W. D. CARÖE, M.A. (Cantab.), Fellow of the Royal Institute of British Architects, and E. J. A. GORDON. With 17 Plates and 32 Illustrations in the Text. Royal 8vo., 31s. 6d.

Joyce.—A SHORT HISTORY OF IRELAND, from the Earliest Times to 1608. By P. W. JOYCE, LL.D. Crown 8vo., 10s. 6d.

Lang.—A HISTORY OF ST. ANDREWS. By ANDREW LANG. With Illustrations by T. HODGE. [*In the Press.*

Lecky.—Works by WILLIAM EDWARD HARTPOLE LECKY.

HISTORY OF ENGLAND IN THE EIGHTEENTH CENTURY.
Library Edition. 8 vols. 8vo., £7 4s.
Cabinet Edition. ENGLAND. 7 vols. Cr. 8vo., 6s. each. IRELAND. 5 vols. Crown 8vo., 6s. each.

HISTORY OF EUROPEAN MORALS FROM AUGUSTUS TO CHARLEMAGNE. 2 vols. Crown 8vo., 16s.

HISTORY OF THE RISE AND INFLUENCE OF THE SPIRIT OF RATIONALISM IN EUROPE. 2 vols. Crown 8vo., 16s.

History, Politics, Polity, and Political Memoirs—*continued.*

Macaulay.—Works by LORD MACAULAY.

COMPLETE WORKS.
  Cabinet Ed. 16 vols. Pt. 8vo., £4 16s.
  Library Edition. 8 vols. 8vo., £5 5s.

HISTORY OF ENGLAND FROM THE ACCESSION OF JAMES THE SECOND.
  Popular Edition. 2 vols. Cr. 8vo., 5s.
  Student's Edition. 2 vols. Cr. 8vo., 12s.
  People's Edition. 4 vols. Cr. 8vo., 16s.
  Cabinet Edition. 8 vols. Pt. 8vo., 48s.
  Library Edition. 5 vols. 8vo., £4.

CRITICAL AND HISTORICAL ESSAYS, WITH LAYS OF ANCIENT ROME, in 1 volume.
  Popular Edition. Crown 8vo., 2s. 6d.
  Authorised Edition. Crown 8vo., 2s. 6d., or 3s. 6d., gilt edges.
  Silver Library Edition. Crown 8vo., 3s. 6d.

CRITICAL AND HISTORICAL ESSAYS.
  Student's Edition. 1 vol. Cr. 8vo., 6s.
  People's Edition. 2 vols. Cr. 8vo., 8s.
  Trevelyan Edition. 2 vols. Cr. 8vo., 9s.
  Cabinet Edition. 4 vols. Post 8vo., 24s.
  Library Edition. 3 vols. 8vo., 36s.

ESSAYS which may be had separately price 6d. each sewed, 1s. each cloth.

Frederick the Great.
Lord Bacon.
Addison and Walpole.
Croker's Boswell's Johnson.
Hallam's Constitutional History.
Warren Hastings (3d. swd., 6d. cl.).
Lord Clive.
The Earl of Chatham (Two Essays).
Ranke and Gladstone.
Milton and Machiavelli.
Lord Byron, and The Comic Dramatists of the Restoration.

SPEECHES. Crown 8vo., 3s. 6d.

MISCELLANEOUS WRITINGS.
  People's Ed. 1 vol. Cr. 8vo., 4s. 6d.
  Library Edition. 2 vols. 8vo., 21s.

MISCELLANEOUS WRITINGS AND SPEECHES.
  Popular Edition. Cr. 8vo., 2s. 6d.
  Student's Edition. Crown 8vo., 6s.
  Cabinet Edition. Including Indian Penal Code, Lays of Ancient Rome, and Miscellaneous Poems. 4 vols. Post 8vo., 24s.

Macaulay.—Works by LORD MACAULAY.—*continued.*

SELECTIONS FROM THE WRITINGS OF LORD MACAULAY. Edited, with Occasional Notes, by the Right Hon. Sir G. O. Trevelyan, Bart. Crown 8vo., 6s.

May.—THE CONSTITUTIONAL HISTORY OF ENGLAND since the Accession of George III. 1760-1870. By Sir THOMAS ERSKINE MAY, K.C.B. (Lord Farnborough). 3 vols. Crown 8vo., 18s.

Merivale.—Works by the Very Rev. CHARLES MERIVALE, Dean of Ely.

HISTORY OF THE ROMANS UNDER THE EMPIRE.
  Cabinet Edition. 8 vols. Cr. 8vo., 48s.
  Silver Library Edition. 8 vols. Cr. 8vo., 3s. 6d. each.

THE FALL OF THE ROMAN REPUBLIC: a Short History of the Last Century of the Commonwealth. 12mo., 7s. 6d.

Parkes.—FIFTY YEARS IN THE MAKING OF AUSTRALIAN HISTORY. By Sir HENRY PARKES, G.C.M.G. With 2 Portraits (1854 and 1892). 2 vols. 8vo., 32s.

Prendergast.—IRELAND FROM THE RESTORATION TO THE REVOLUTION, 1660-1690. By JOHN P. PRENDERGAST, Author of 'The Cromwellian Settlement in Ireland'. 8vo., 5s.

Round.—GEOFFREY DE MANDEVILLE: a Study of the Anarchy. By J. H. ROUND, M.A. 8vo., 16s.

Seebohm.—THE ENGLISH VILLAGE COMMUNITY Examined in its Relations to the Manorial and Tribal Systems, &c. By FREDERIC SEEBOHM. With 13 Maps and Plates. 8vo., 16s.

Smith.—CARTHAGE AND THE CARTHAGINIANS. By R. BOSWORTH SMITH, M.A., Assistant Master in Harrow School. With Maps, Plans, &c. Cr. 8vo., 6s.

Stephens.—PAROCHIAL SELF-GOVERNMENT IN RURAL DISTRICTS: Argument and Plan. By HENRY C. STEPHENS, M.P. 4to., 12s. 6d. Popular Edition. Cr. 8vo., 1s.

History, Politics, Polity, and Political Memoirs—*continued*.

Stephens.—A HISTORY OF THE FRENCH REVOLUTION. By H. MORSE STEPHENS, Balliol College, Oxford. 3 vols. 8vo. Vols. I. and II. 18*s.* each.

Stubbs.—HISTORY OF THE UNIVERSITY OF DUBLIN, from its Foundation to the End of the Eighteenth Century. By J. W. STUBBS. 8vo., 12*s.* 6*d.*

Thompson.—POLITICS IN A DEMOCRACY: an Essay. By DANIEL GREENLEAF THOMPSON, Author of 'A System of Psychology, &c. Cr. 8vo., 5*s.*

Todd.—PARLIAMENTARY GOVERNMENT IN THE COLONIES. By ALPHEUS TODD, LL.D. [*In the Press.*

Tupper.—OUR INDIAN PROTECTORATE: an Introduction to the Study of the Relations between the British Government and its Indian Feudatories. By CHARLES LEWIS TUPPER, Indian Civil Service. Royal 8vo., 16*s.*

Wakeman and Hassall.—ESSAYS INTRODUCTORY TO THE STUDY OF ENGLISH CONSTITUTIONAL HISTORY. By Resident Members of the University of Oxford. Edited by HENRY OFFLEY WAKEMAN, M.A., and ARTHUR HASSALL, M.A. Crown 8vo., 6*s.*

Walpole.—Works by SPENCER WALPOLE.
HISTORY OF ENGLAND FROM THE CONCLUSION OF THE GREAT WAR IN 1815 TO 1858. 6 vols. Crown 8vo., 6*s.* each.
THE LAND OF HOME RULE: being an Account of the History and Institutions of the Isle of Man. Cr. 8vo., 6*s.*

Wylie.—HISTORY OF ENGLAND UNDER HENRY IV. By JAMES HAMILTON WYLIE, M.A., one of H. M. Inspectors of Schools. 3 vols. Vol. I., 1399-1404. Crown 8vo., 10*s.* 6*d.* Vol. II. [*In the Press.* Vol. III. [*In preparation.*

Biography, Personal Memoirs, &c.

Armstrong.—THE LIFE AND LETTERS OF EDMUND J. ARMSTRONG. Edited by G. F. ARMSTRONG. Fcp. 8vo., 7*s.* 6*d.*

Bacon.—LETTERS AND LIFE, INCLUDING ALL HIS OCCASIONAL WORKS. Edited by J. SPEDDING. 7 vols. 8vo., £4 4*s.*

Bagehot.—BIOGRAPHICAL STUDIES. By WALTER BAGEHOT. 8vo., 12*s.*

Boyd.—TWENTY-FIVE YEARS OF ST. ANDREWS, 1865-1890. By A. K. H. BOYD, D.D., Author of 'Recreations of a Country Parson,' &c. 2 vols. 8vo. Vol. I., 12*s.* Vol. II., 15*s.*

Carlyle.—THOMAS CARLYLE: a History of his Life. By J. A. FROUDE.
1795-1835. 2 vols. Crown 8vo., 7*s.*
1834-1881. 2 vols. Crown 8vo., 7*s.*

Fabert.—ABRAHAM FABERT: Governor of Sedan and Marshal of France. His Life and Times, 1599-1662. By GEORGE HOOPER, Author of 'Waterloo,' 'Wellington,' &c. With a Portrait. 8vo., 10*s.* 6*d.*

Fox.—THE EARLY HISTORY OF CHARLES JAMES FOX. By the Right Hon. Sir G. O. TREVELYAN, Bart.
Library Edition. 8vo., 18*s.*
Cabinet Edition. Crown 8vo., 6*s.*

Hamilton.—LIFE OF SIR WILLIAM HAMILTON. By R. P. GRAVES. 3 vols. 15*s.* each.
ADDENDUM TO THE LIFE OF SIR WM. ROWAN HAMILTON, LL.D., D.C.L., 8vo., 6*d.* sewed.

Hassall.—THE NARRATIVE OF A BUSY LIFE: an Autobiography. By ARTHUR HILL HASSALL, M.D. 8vo., 5*s.*

Havelock.—MEMOIRS OF SIR HENRY HAVELOCK, K.C.B. By JOHN CLARK MARSHMAN. Crown 8vo., 3*s.* 6*d.*

Macaulay.—THE LIFE AND LETTERS OF LORD MACAULAY. By the Right Hon. Sir G. O. TREVELYAN, Bart.
Popular Edition. 1 vol. Cr. 8vo.,2*s.* 6*d.*
Student's Edition. 1 vol. Cr. 8vo., 6*s.*
Cabinet Edition. 2 vols. Post 8vo., 12*s.*
Library Edition. 2 vols. 8vo., 36*s.*

Marbot.—THE MEMOIRS OF THE BARON DE MARBOT. Translated from the French by ARTHUR JOHN BUTLER, M.A. Crown 8vo., 7*s.* 6*d.*

Montrose.—DEEDS OF MONTROSE: THE MEMOIRS OF JAMES, MARQUIS OF MONTROSE, 1639-1650. By the Rev. GEORGE WISHART, D.D. (Bishop of Edinburgh, 1662-1671). Translated, with Introduction, Notes, &c., and the original Latin, by the Rev. ALEXANDER MURDOCH, F.S.A. (Scot.), and H. F. MORELAND SIMPSON, M.A. (Cantab.). 4to., 36*s.* net.

Biography, Personal Memoirs, &c.—*continued*.

Seebohm.—THE OXFORD REFORMERS —JOHN COLET, ERASMUS AND THOMAS MORE : a History of their Fellow-Work. By FREDERIC SEEBOHM. 8vo., 14*s*.

Shakespeare.—OUTLINES OF THE LIFE OF SHAKESPEARE. By J. O. HALLIWELL-PHILLIPPS. With numerous Illustrations and Fac-similes. 2 vols. Royal 8vo., £1 1*s*.

Shakespeare's TRUE LIFE. By JAS. WALTER. With 500 Illustrations by GERALD E. MOIRA. Imp. 8vo., 21*s*.

Sherbrooke.—LIFE AND LETTERS OF THE RIGHT HON. ROBERT LOWE, VISCOUNT SHERBROOKE, G.C.B., together with a Memoir of his Kinsman, Sir JOHN COAPE SHERBROOKE, G.C.B. By A. PATCHETT MARTIN. With 5 Portraits. 2 vols. 8vo., 36*s*.

Stephen.—ESSAYS IN ECCLESIASTICAL BIOGRAPHY. By Sir JAMES STEPHEN. Crown 8vo., 7*s*. 6*d*.

Verney.—MEMOIRS OF THE VERNEY FAMILY DURING THE CIVIL WAR. Compiled from the Letters and Illustrated by the Portraits at Claydon House, Bucks. By FRANCES PARTHENOPE VERNEY. With a Preface by S. R. GARDINER, M.A., LL.D. With 38 Portraits, Woodcuts and Fac-simile. 2 vols. Royal 8vo., 42*s*.

Wagner.—WAGNER AS I KNEW HIM. By FERDINAND PRAEGER. Crown 8vo., 7*s*. 6*d*.

Walford.—TWELVE ENGLISH AUTHORESSES. By L. B. WALFORD, Author of 'Mischief of Monica,' &c. With Portrait of Hannah More. Crown 8vo., 4*s*. 6*d*.

Wellington.—LIFE OF THE DUKE OF WELLINGTON. By the Rev. G. R. GLEIG, M.A. Crown 8vo., 3*s*. 6*d*.

Wordsworth.—Works by CHARLES WORDSWORTH, D.C.L., late Bishop of St. Andrews.

ANNALS OF MY EARLY LIFE, 1806-1846. 8vo., 15*s*.

ANNALS OF MY LIFE, 1847-1856. 8vo., 10*s*. 6*d*.

Travel and Adventure.

Arnold.—SEAS AND LANDS. By Sir EDWIN ARNOLD, K.C.I.E., Author of 'The Light of the World,' &c. Reprinted Letters from the 'Daily Telegraph.' With 71 Illustrations. Cr. 8vo., 7*s*. 6*d*.

Baker.—Works by Sir SAMUEL WHITE BAKER.

EIGHT YEARS IN CEYLON. With 6 Illustrations. Crown 8vo., 3*s*. 6*d*.

THE RIFLE AND THE HOUND IN CEYLON. 6 Illustrations. Cr. 8vo., 3*s*. 6*d*.

Bent.—Works by J. THEODORE BENT, F.S.A., F.R.G.S.

THE RUINED CITIES OF MASHONALAND : being a Record of Excavation and Exploration in 1891. With Map, 13 Plates, and 104 Illustrations in the Text. Cr. 8vo., 7*s*. 6*d*.

THE SACRED CITY OF THE ETHIOPIANS: being a Record of Travel and Research in Abyssinia in 1893. With 8 Plates and 65 Illustrations in the Text. 8vo.

Brassey.—Works by LADY BRASSEY.

A VOYAGE IN THE 'SUNBEAM'; OUR HOME ON THE OCEAN FOR ELEVEN MONTHS.

Library Edition. With 8 Maps and Charts, and 118 Illustrations. 8vo., 21*s*.

Cabinet Edition. With Map and 66 Illustrations. Crown 8vo., 7*s*. 6*d*.

Silver Library Edition. With 66 Illustrations. Crown 8vo., 3*s*. 6*d*.

Popular Edition. With 60 Illustrations. 4to., 6*d*. sewed, 1*s*. cloth.

School Edition. With 37 Illustrations. Fcp., 2*s*. cloth, or 3*s*. white parchment.

THREE VOYAGES IN THE 'SUNBEAM'. Popular Edition. With 346 Illustrations. 4to., 2*s*. 6*d*.

Travel and Adventure—*continued*.

Brassey.—Works by LADY BRASSEY—*cont.*
  SUNSHINE AND STORM IN THE EAST.
    Library Edition. With 2 Maps and 141 Illustrations. 8vo., 21*s.*
    Cabinet Edition. With 2 Maps and 114 Illustrations. Crown 8vo., 7*s.* 6*d.*
    Popular Edition. With 103 Illustrations. 4to., 6*d.* sewed, 1*s.* cloth.
  THE LAST VOYAGE TO INDIA AND AUSTRALIA IN THE 'SUNBEAM'. With Charts and Maps, and 40 Illustrations in Monotone (20 full-page), and nearly 200 Illustrations in the Text from Drawings by R. T. PRITCHETT. 8vo., 21*s.*
  IN THE TRADES, THE TROPICS, AND THE 'ROARING FORTIES'.
    Cabinet Edition. With Map and 220 Illustrations. Crown 8vo., 7*s.* 6*d.*
    Popular Edition. With 183 Illustrations. 4to., 6*d.* sewed, 1*s.* cloth.

Curzon.—PERSIA AND THE PERSIAN QUESTION. With 9 Maps, 96 Illustrations, Appendices, and an Index. By the Hon. GEORGE N. CURZON, M.P., late Fellow of All Souls' College, Oxford. 2 vols. 8vo., 42*s.*

Froude.—Works by JAMES A. FROUDE.
  OCEANA: or England and her Colonies. With 9 Illustrations. Crown 8vo., 2*s.* boards, 2*s.* 6*d.* cloth.
  THE ENGLISH IN THE WEST INDIES: or the Bow of Ulysses. With 9 Illustrations. Cr. 8vo., 2*s.* bds., 2*s.* 6*d.* cl.

Howard.—LIFE WITH TRANS-SIBERIAN SAVAGES. By B. DOUGLAS HOWARD, M.A. Crown 8vo., 6*s.*

Howells.—VENETIAN LIFE. By WILLIAM DEAN HOWELLS. With 18 Illustrations in aqua-tint from original Water Colours. 2 vols. Crown 8vo., 21*s.*

Howitt.—VISITS TO REMARKABLE PLACES, Old Halls, Battle-Fjelds, Scenes illustrative of Striking Passages in English History and Poetry. By WILLIAM HOWITT. With 80 Illustrations. Crown 8vo., 3*s.* 6*d.*

Knight.—Works by E. F. KNIGHT, Author of the Cruise of the 'Falcon'.
  THE CRUISE OF THE 'ALERTE': the Narrative of a Search for Treasure on the Desert Island of Trinidad. With 2 Maps and 23 Illustrations. Crown 8vo., 3*s.* 6*d.* [*Continued.*

Knight.—Works by E.F.KNIGHT—*cont.*
  WHERE THREE EMPIRES MEET: a Narrative of Recent Travel in Kashmir, Western Tibet, Baltistan, Ladak, Gilgit, and the adjoining Countries. With a Map and 54 Illustrations. Cr. 8vo., 7*s.* 6*d.*

Lees and Clutterbuck.—B. C. 1887: A RAMBLE IN BRITISH COLUMBIA. By J. A. LEES and W. J. CLUTTERBUCK, Authors of 'Three in Norway'. With Map and 75 Illustrations. Cr. 8vo., 3*s.* 6*d.*

Nansen.—Works by Dr. FRIDTJOF NANSEN.
  THE FIRST CROSSING OF GREENLAND. With numerous Illustrations and a Map. Crown 8vo., 7*s.* 6*d.*
  ESKIMO LIFE. Translated by WILLIAM ARCHER. With 16 Plates and 15 Illustrations in the Text. 8vo., 16*s.*

Pratt.—TO THE SNOWS OF TIBET THROUGH CHINA. By A. E. PRATT, F.R.G.S. With 33 Illustrations and a Map. 8vo., 18*s.*

Riley.—ATHOS: or the Mountain of the Monks. By ATHELSTAN RILEY, M.A. With Map and 29 Illustrations. 8vo., 21*s.*

Stephens.—MADOC: An Essay on the Discovery of America, by MADOC AP OWEN GWYNEDD, in the Twelfth Century. By THOMAS STEPHENS. Edited by LLYWARCH REYNOLDS, B.A. Oxon. 8vo., 7*s.* 6*d.*

Von Hohnel.—DISCOVERY OF LAKES RUDOLF AND STEFANIE: Account of Count SAMUEL TELEKI'S Exploring and Hunting Expedition in Eastern Equatorial Africa in 1887 and 1888. By his companion, Lieutenant LUDWIG VON HOHNEL. Translated by NANCY BELL (N. D'ANVERS). With 179 Illustrations, 2 Large and 4 Small Coloured Maps, giving Route of Expedition. 2 vols. 8vo., 42*s.*

THREE IN NORWAY. By Two of Them. With a Map and 59 Illustrations. Cr. 8vo., 2*s.* boards, 2*s.* 6*d.* cloth.

Whishaw.—OUT OF DOORS IN TSARLAND; a Record of the Seeings and Doings of a Wanderer in Russia. By FRED. J. WHISHAW. Cr. 8vo., 7*s.* 6*d.*

Wolff.—Works by HENRY W. WOLFF.
  RAMBLES IN THE BLACK FOREST. Crown 8vo., 7*s.* 6*d.*
  THE WATERING PLACES OF THE VOSGES. Crown 8vo., 4*s.* 6*d.*
  THE COUNTRY OF THE VOSGES. With a Map. 8vo., 12*s.*

Sport and Pastime.
THE BADMINTON LIBRARY.

Edited by the DUKE OF BEAUFORT, K.G., assisted by ALFRED E. T. WATSON.

ATHLETICS AND FOOTBALL. By MONTAGUE SHEARMAN. With 51 Illustrations. Crown 8vo., 10s. 6d.

BIG GAME SHOOTING. By C. PHILLIPPS-WOLLEY, F. C. SELONS, W. G. LITTLEDALE, Colonel PERCY, FRED. JACKSON, Major H. PERCY, W. C. OSWELL, Sir HENRY POTTINGER, Bart., and the EARL OF KILMOREY. With Contributions by other Writers. With Illustrations by CHARLES WHYMPER and others. 2 vols. [*In the Press.*

BOATING. By W. B. WOODGATE. With an Introduction by the Rev. EDMOND WARRE, D.D., and a Chapter on 'Rowing at Eton,' by R. HARVEY MASON. With 49 Illustrations. Cr. 8vo., 10s. 6d.

COURSING AND FALCONRY. By HARDING COX and the Hon. GERALD LASCELLES. With 76 Illustrations. Crown 8vo., 10s. 6d.

CRICKET. By A. G. STEEL and the Hon. R. H. LYTTELTON. With Contributions by ANDREW LANG, R. A. H. MITCHELL, W. G. GRACE, and F. GALE. With 63 Illustrations. Cr. 8vo., 10s. 6d.

CYCLING. By VISCOUNT BURY (Earl of Albemarle), K.C.M.G., and G. LACY HILLIER. With 89 Illustrations. Crown 8vo., 10s. 6d.

DRIVING. By the DUKE OF BEAUFORT. With 65 Illustrations. Cr. 8vo., 10s. 6d.

FENCING, BOXING, AND WRESTLING. By WALTER H. POLLOCK, F. C. GROVE, C. PREVOST, E. B. MITCHELL, and WALTER ARMSTRONG. With 42 Illustrations. Crown 8vo., 10s. 6d.

FISHING. By H. CHOLMONDELEY-PENNELL. With Contributions by the MARQUIS OF EXETER, HENRY R. FRANCIS, Major JOHN P. TRAHERNE, FREDERIC M. HALFORD, G. CHRISTOPHER DAVIES, R. B. MARSTON, &c.

Vol. I. Salmon, Trout, and Grayling. With 158 Illustrations. Crown 8vo., 10s. 6d.

Vol. II. Pike and other Coarse Fish. With 133 Illustrations. Crown 8vo., 10s. 6d.

GOLF. By HORACE G. HUTCHINSON, the Rt. Hon. A. J. BALFOUR, M.P., Sir W. G. SIMPSON, Bart., LORD WELLWOOD, H. S. C. EVERARD, ANDREW LANG, and other Writers. With 91 Illustrations. Cr. 8vo., 10s. 6d.

HUNTING. By the DUKE OF BEAUFORT, K.G., and MOWBRAY MORRIS. With Contributions by the EARL OF SUFFOLK AND BERKSHIRE, Rev. E. W. L. DAVIES, DIGBY COLLINS and ALFRED E. T. WATSON. With 53 Illustrations. Crown 8vo., 10s. 6d.

MOUNTAINEERING. By C. T. DENT, Sir F. POLLOCK, Bart., W. M. CONWAY, DOUGLAS FRESHFIELD, C. E. MATHEWS, C. PILKINGTON, and other Writers. With 108 Illustrations. Cr. 8vo., 10s. 6d.

RACING AND STEEPLE-CHASING. *Racing:* By the EARL OF SUFFOLK AND BERKSHIRE and W. G. CRAVEN. With a Contribution by the Hon. F. LAWLEY. *Steeple-chasing:* By ARTHUR COVENTRY and ALFRED E. T. WATSON. With 58 Illusts. Cr. 8vo., 10s. 6d.

RIDING AND POLO. By Captain ROBERT WEIR, J. MORAY BROWN, the DUKE OF BEAUFORT, K.G., the EARL of SUFFOLK AND BERKSHIRE, &c. With 59 Illustrations. Cr. 8vo., 10s. 6d.

SHOOTING. By Lord WALSINGHAM and Sir RALPH PAYNE-GALLWEY, Bart. With Contributions by LORD LOVAT, LORD CHARLES LENNOX KERR, the Hon. G. LASCELLES, and A. J. STUART-WORTLEY.

Vol I. Field and Covert. With 105 Illustrations. Crown 8vo., 10s. 6d.

Vol. II. Moor and Marsh. With 65 Illustrations. Cr. 8vo., 10s. 6d.

SKATING, CURLING, TOBOGANING, AND OTHER ICE SPORTS. By JN. M. HEATHCOTE, C. G. TEBBUTT, T. MAXWELL WITHAM, the Rev. JOHN KERR, ORMOND HAKE, and Colonel BUCK. With 284 Illustrations. Cr. 8vo., 10s. 6d.

SWIMMING. By ARCHIBALD SINCLAIR and WILLIAM HENRY, Hon. Secs. of the Life Saving Society. With 119 Illustrations. Cr. 8vo., 10s. 6d.

[*Continued.*

Sport and Pastime—*continued.*

THE BADMINTON LIBRARY—*continued.*

TENNIS, LAWN TENNIS, RACQUETS, AND FIVES. By J. M. and C. G. HEATHCOTE, E. O. PLEYDELL-BOUVERIE and A. C. AINGER. With Contributions by the Hon. A. LYTTELTON, W. C. MARSHALL, Miss L. DOD, H. W. W. WILBERFORCE, H. F. LAWFORD, &c. With 79 Illustrations. Crown 8vo., 10s. 6d.

YACHTING. By the EARL OF PEMBROKE, the MARQUIS OF DUFFERIN AND AVA, the EARL OF ONSLOW, LORD BRASSEY Lieut.-Col. BUCKNILL, LEWIS HERRESHOFF, G. L. WATSON, E. F. KNIGHT, Rev. G. L. BLAKE, R.N., and G. C. DAVIES. With Illustrations by R. T. PRITCHETT, and from Photographs. 2 vols. [*In the Press.*

Campbell-Walker.—THE CORRECT CARD: or, How to Play at Whist; a Whist Catechism. By Major A. CAMPBELL-WALKER, F.R.G.S. Fcp. 8vo., 2s. 6d.

DEAD SHOT (THE): or, Sportsman's Complete Guide. Being a Treatise on the Use of the Gun, with Rudimentary and Finishing Lessons on the Art of Shooting Game of all kinds, also Game Driving, Wild-Fowl and Pigeon Shooting, Dog Breaking, etc. By MARKSMAN. Crown 8vo., 10s. 6d.

Falkener.—GAMES, ANCIENT AND ORIENTAL, AND HOW TO PLAY THEM. Being the Games of the Ancient Egyptians, the Hiera Gramme of the Greeks, the Ludus Latrunculorum of the Romans, and the Oriental Games of Chess, Draughts, Backgammon, and Magic Squares. By EDWARD FALKENER. With numerous Photographs, Diagrams, &c. 8vo., 21s.

Ford.—THE THEORY AND PRACTICE OF ARCHERY. By HORACE FORD. New Edition, thoroughly Revised and Rewritten by W. BUTT, M.A. With a Preface by C. J. LONGMAN, M.A. 8vo., 14s.

Francis.—A BOOK ON ANGLING: or, Treatise on the Art of Fishing in every Branch; including full Illustrated List of Salmon Flies. By FRANCIS FRANCIS. With Coloured Plates. Cr. 8vo., 15s.

Hawker.—THE DIARY OF COLONEL PETER HAWKER, author of "Instructions to Young Sportsmen". With an Introduction by Sir RALPH PAYNE-GALLWEY, Bart. With 2 Portraits of the Author and 8 Illustrations. 2 vols. 8vo., 32s.

Hopkins.—FISHING REMINISCENCES. By Major E. P. HOPKINS. With Illustrations. Crown 8vo., 6s. 6d.

Lang.—ANGLING SKETCHES. By ANDREW LANG. With 20 Illustrations. Crown 8vo., 7s. 6d.

Longman.—CHESS OPENINGS. By FRED. W. LONGMAN. Fcp. 8vo., 2s. 6d.

Payne-Gallwey.—Works by Sir RALPH PAYNE-GALLWEY, Bart.
LETTERS TO YOUNG SHOOTERS (First Series). On the Choice and Use of a Gun. With Illustrations. Crown 8vo., 7s. 6d.
LETTERS TO YOUNG SHOOTERS. (Second Series). On the Production, Preservation, and Killing of Game. With Directions in Shooting Wood-Pigeons and Breaking-in Retrievers. With 103 Illustrations. Crown 8vo., 12s. 6d.

Pole.—THE THEORY OF THE MODERN SCIENTIFIC GAME OF WHIST. By W. POLE, F.R.S. Fcp. 8vo., 2s. 6d.

Proctor.—Works by RICHARD A. PROCTOR.
HOW TO PLAY WHIST: WITH THE LAWS AND ETIQUETTE OF WHIST. Crown 8vo., 3s. 6d.
HOME WHIST: an Easy Guide to Correct Play. 16mo., 1s.

Ronalds.—THE FLY-FISHER'S ENTOMOLOGY. By ALFRED RONALDS. With 20 Coloured Plates. 8vo., 14s.

Wilcocks. THE SEA FISHERMAN: Comprising the Chief Methods of Hook and Line Fishing in the British and other Seas, and Remarks on Nets, Boats, and Boating. By J. C. WILCOCKS. Illustrated. Crown 8vo., 6s.

Mental, Moral, and Political Philosophy.

LOGIC, RHETORIC, PSYCHOLOGY, ETC.

Abbott.—THE ELEMENTS OF LOGIC. By T. K. ABBOTT, B.D. 12mo., 3s.

Aristotle.—Works by.

THE POLITICS: G. Bekker's Greek Text of Books I., III., IV. (VII.), with an English Translation by W. E. BOLLAND, M.A.; and short Introductory Essays by A. LANG, M.A. Crown 8vo., 7s. 6d.

THE POLITICS: Introductory Essays. By ANDREW LANG (from Bolland and Lang's 'Politics'). Cr. 8vo., 2s. 6d.

THE ETHICS: Greek Text, Illustrated with Essay and Notes. By Sir ALEXANDER GRANT, Bart. 2 vols. 8vo., 32s.

THE NICOMACHEAN ETHICS: Newly Translated into English. By ROBERT WILLIAMS. Crown 8vo., 7s. 6d.

AN INTRODUCTION TO ARISTOTLE'S ETHICS. Books I.-IV. (Book X. c. vi.-ix. in an Appendix.) With a continuous Analysis and Notes. Intended for the use of Beginners and Junior Students. By the Rev. EDWARD MOORE, D.D., Principal of St. Edmund Hall, and late Fellow and Tutor of Queen's College, Oxford. Crown 8vo., 10s. 6d.

Bacon.—Works by.

COMPLETE WORKS. Edited by R. L. ELLIS, J. SPEDDING, and D. D. HEATH. 7 vols. 8vo., £3 13s. 6d.

THE ESSAYS: with Annotations. By RICHARD WHATELY, D.D. 8vo. 10s. 6d.

Bain.—Works by ALEXANDER BAIN, LL.D.

MENTAL SCIENCE. Crown 8vo., 6s. 6d.

MORAL SCIENCE. Crown 8vo., 4s. 6d.

The two works as above can be had in one volume, price 10s. 6d.

SENSES AND THE INTELLECT. 8vo., 15s.

EMOTIONS AND THE WILL. 8vo., 15s.

LOGIC, DEDUCTIVE AND INDUCTIVE. Part I., 4s. Part II., 6s. 6d.

PRACTICAL ESSAYS. Crown 8vo., 2s.

Bray.—Works by CHARLES BRAY.

THE PHILOSOPHY OF NECESSITY: or Law in Mind as in Matter. Cr. 8vo., 5s.

THE EDUCATION OF THE FEELINGS: a Moral System for Schools. Crown 8vo., 2s. 6d.

Bray.—ELEMENTS OF MORALITY, in Easy Lessons for Home and School Teaching. By Mrs. CHARLES BRAY. Cr. 8vo., 1s. 6d.

Crozier.—CIVILISATION AND PROGRESS. By JOHN BEATTIE CROZIER, M.D. With New Preface, more fully explaining the nature of the New Organon used in the solution of its problems. 8vo., 14s.

Davidson.—THE LOGIC OF DEFINITION, Explained and Applied. By WILLIAM L. DAVIDSON, M.A. Crown 8vo., 6s.

Green.—THE WORKS OF THOMAS HILL GREEN. Edited by R. L. NETTLESHIP.

Vols. I. and II. Philosophical Works. 8vo., 16s. each.

Vol. III. Miscellanies. With Index to the three Volumes, and Memoir. 8vo., 21s.

Hearn.—THE ARYAN HOUSEHOLD: its Structure and its Development. An Introduction to Comparative Jurisprudence. By W. EDWARD HEARN. 8vo., 16s.

Hodgson.—Works by SHADWORTH H. HODGSON.

TIME AND SPACE: a Metaphysical Essay. 8vo., 16s.

THE THEORY OF PRACTICE: an Ethical Inquiry. 2 vols. 8vo., 24s.

THE PHILOSOPHY OF REFLECTION. 2 vols. 8vo., 21s.

Hume.—THE PHILOSOPHICAL WORKS OF DAVID HUME. Edited by T. H. GREEN and T. H. GROSE. 4 vols. 8vo., 56s. Or separately, Essays. 2 vols. 28s. Treatise of Human Nature. 2 vols. 28s.

Mental, Moral and Political Philosophy—*continued*.

Johnstone—A SHORT INTRODUCTION TO THE STUDY OF LOGIC. By LAURENCE JOHNSTONE. With Questions. Cr. 8vo., 2s. 6d.

Jones.—AN INTRODUCTION TO GENERAL LOGIC. By E. E. CONSTANCE JONES, Author of 'Elements of Logic as a Science of Propositions'. Cr. 8vo., 4s. 6d.

Justinian.—THE INSTITUTES OF JUSTINIAN: Latin Text, chiefly that of Huschke, with English Introduction, Translation, Notes, and Summary. By THOMAS C. SANDARS, M.A. 8vo. 18s.

Kant.—Works by IMMANUEL KANT.

CRITIQUE OF PRACTICAL REASON, AND OTHER WORKS ON THE THEORY OF ETHICS. Translated by T. K. ABBOTT, B.D. With Memoir. 8vo., 12s. 6d.

INTRODUCTION TO LOGIC, AND HIS ESSAY ON THE MISTAKEN SUBTILTY OF THE FOUR FIGURES. Translated by T. K. ABBOTT, and with Notes by S. T. COLERIDGE. 8vo., 6s.

Killick.—HANDBOOK TO MILL'S SYSTEM OF LOGIC. By Rev. A. H. KILLICK, M.A. Crown 8vo., 3s. 6d.

Ladd.—Works by GEORGE TURNBULL LADD.

ELEMENTS OF PHYSIOLOGICAL PSYCHOLOGY. 8vo., 21s.

OUTLINES OF PHYSIOLOGICAL PSYCHOLOGY. A Text-Book of Mental Science for Academies and Colleges. 8vo., 12s.

Lewes.—THE HISTORY OF PHILOSOPHY, from Thales to Comte. By GEORGE HENRY LEWES. 2 vols. 8vo., 32s.

Max Müller.—Works by F. MAX MÜLLER.

THE SCIENCE OF THOUGHT. 8vo., 21s.
THREE INTRODUCTORY LECTURES ON THE SCIENCE OF THOUGHT. 8vo., 2s. 6d.

Mill.—ANALYSIS OF THE PHENOMENA OF THE HUMAN MIND. By JAMES MILL. 2 vols. 8vo., 28s.

Mill.—Works by JOHN STUART MILL.

A SYSTEM OF LOGIC. Cr. 8vo., 3s. 6d.
ON LIBERTY. Cr. 8vo., 1s. 4d.
ON REPRESENTATIVE GOVERNMENT. Crown 8vo., 2s.
UTILITARIANISM. 8vo., 5s.
EXAMINATION OF SIR WILLIAM HAMILTON'S PHILOSOPHY. 8vo., 16s.
NATURE, THE UTILITY OF RELIGION, AND THEISM. Three Essays. 8vo., 5s.

Monck.—INTRODUCTION TO LOGIC. By H. S. MONCK. Crown 8vo., 5s.

Ribot.—THE PSYCHOLOGY OF ATTENTION. By TH. RIBOT. Cr. 8vo., 3s.

Sidgwick.—DISTINCTION: and the Criticism of Belief. By ALFRED SIDGWICK. Crown 8vo., 6s.

Stock.—DEDUCTIVE LOGIC. By ST. GEORGE STOCK. Fcp. 8vo., 3s. 6d.

Sully.—Works by JAMES SULLY, Grote Professor of Mind and Logic at University College, London.

THE HUMAN MIND: a Text-book of Psychology. 2 vols. 8vo., 21s.

OUTLINES OF PSYCHOLOGY. 8vo., 9s.

THE TEACHER'S HANDBOOK OF PSYCHOLOGY. Crown 8vo., 5s.

Swinburne.—PICTURE LOGIC: an Attempt to Popularise the Science of Reasoning. By ALFRED JAMES SWINBURNE, M.A. With 23 Woodcuts. Post 8vo., 5s.

Thompson.—Works by DANIEL GREENLEAF THOMPSON.

A SYSTEM OF PSYCHOLOGY. 2 vols. 8vo., 36s.

THE RELIGIOUS SENTIMENTS OF THE HUMAN MIND. 8vo., 7s. 6d.

THE PROBLEM OF EVIL: an Introduction to the Practical Sciences. 8vo., 10s. 6d.

Mental, Moral and Political Philosophy—*continued*.

Thompson. — Works by DANIEL GREENLEAF THOMPSON—*continued*.

SOCIAL PROGRESS. 8vo., 7s. 6d.

THE PHILOSOPHY OF FICTION IN LITERATURE. Crown 8vo., 6s.

Thomson.—OUTLINES OF THE NECESSARY LAWS OF THOUGHT: a Treatise on Pure and Applied Logic. By WILLIAM THOMSON, D.D., formerly Lord Archbishop of York. Post 8vo., 6s.

Webb.—THE VEIL OF ISIS: a Series of Essays on Idealism. By T. E. WEBB. 8vo., 10s. 6d.

Whately.—Works by R. WHATELY, formerly Archbishop of Dublin.

BACON'S ESSAYS. With Annotation. By R. WHATELY. 8vo., 10s. 6d.

ELEMENTS OF LOGIC. Cr. 8vo., 4s. 6d.

ELEMENTS OF RHETORIC. Cr. 8vo., 4s. 6d.

LESSONS ON REASONING. Fcp. 8vo., 1s. 6d.

Zeller.—Works by Dr. EDWARD ZELLER, Professor in the University of Berlin.

HISTORY OF ECLECTICISM IN GREEK PHILOSOPHY. Translated by SARAH F. ALLEYNE. Cr. 8vo., 10s. 6d.

THE STOICS, EPICUREANS, AND SCEPTICS. Translated by the Rev. O. J. REICHEL, M.A. Crown 8vo., 15s.

OUTLINES OF THE HISTORY OF GREEK PHILOSOPHY. Translated by SARAH F. ALLEYNE and EVELYN ABBOTT. Crown 8vo., 10s. 6d.

PLATO AND THE OLDER ACADEMY. Translated by SARAH F. ALLEYNE and ALFRED GOODWIN, B.A. Crown 8vo., 18s.

SOCRATES AND THE SOCRATIC SCHOOLS. Translated by the Rev. O. J. REICHEL, M.A. Crown 8vo., 10s. 6d.

THE PRE-SOCRATIC SCHOOLS: a History of Greek Philosophy from the Earliest Period to the time of Socrates. Translated by SARAH F. ALLEYNE. 2 vols. Crown 8vo., 30s.

MANUALS OF CATHOLIC PHILOSOPHY.
(Stonyhurst Series.)

A MANUAL OF POLITICAL ECONOMY. By C. S. DEVAS, M.A. Cr. 8vo., 6s. 6d.

FIRST PRINCIPLES OF KNOWLEDGE. By JOHN RICKABY, S.J. Crown 8vo., 5s.

GENERAL METAPHYSICS. By JOHN RICKABY, S.J. Crown 8vo., 5s.

LOGIC. By RICHARD F. CLARKE, S.J. Crown 8vo., 5s.

MORAL PHILOSOPHY (ETHICS AND NATURAL LAW. By JOSEPH RICKABY, S.J. Crown 8vo., 5s.

NATURAL THEOLOGY. By BERNARD BOEDDER, S.J. Crown 8vo., 6s. 6d.

PSYCHOLOGY. By MICHAEL MAHER, S.J. Crown 8vo., 6s. 6d.

History and Science of Language, &c.

Davidson.—LEADING AND IMPORTANT ENGLISH WORDS: Explained and Exemplified. By WILLIAM L. DAVIDSON, M.A. Fcp. 8vo., 3s. 6d.

Farrar.—LANGUAGE AND LANGUAGES: By F. W. FARRAR, D.D., F.R.S., Cr. 8vo., 6s.

Graham.—ENGLISH SYNONYMS, Classified and Explained: with Practical Exercises. By G. F. GRAHAM. Fcp. 8vo., 6s.

Max Müller.—Works by F. MAX MÜLLER.

SELECTED ESSAYS ON LANGUAGE, MYTHOLOGY, AND RELIGION. 2 vols. Crown 8vo., 16s. [*Continued.*

History and Science of Language, &c.—*continued*.

Max Müller.—Works by F. MAX MÜLLER—*continued*.

   THE SCIENCE OF LANGUAGE, Founded on Lectures delivered at the Royal Institution in 1861 and 1863. 2 vols. Crown 8vo., 21s.

   BIOGRAPHIES OF WORDS, AND THE HOME OF THE ARYAS. Crown 8vo., 7s. 6d.

   THREE LECTURES ON THE SCIENCE OF LANGUAGE, AND ITS PLACE IN GENERAL EDUCATION, delivered at Oxford, 1889. Crown 8vo., 3s.

Roget.—THESAURUS OF ENGLISH WORDS AND PHRASES. Classified and Arranged so as to Facilitate the Expression of Ideas and assist in Literary Composition. By PETER MARK ROGET, M.D., F.R.S. Recomposed throughout, enlarged and improved, partly from the Author's Notes, and with a full Index, by the Author's Son, JOHN LEWIS ROGET. Crown 8vo., 10s. 6d.

Strong, Logeman, and Wheeler. INTRODUCTION TO THE STUDY OF THE HISTORY OF LANGUAGE. By HERBERT A. STRONG. M.A., LL.D., WILLEM S. LOGEMAN, and BENJAMIN IDE WHEELER. 8vo., 10s. 6d.

Whately.—ENGLISH SYNONYMS. By E. JANE WHATELY. Fcp. 8vo., 3s.

Political Economy and Economics.

Ashley.—ENGLISH ECONOMIC HISTORY AND THEORY. By W. J. ASHLEY, M.A. Crown 8vo., Part I., 5s. Part II., 10s. 6d.

Bagehot.—ECONOMIC STUDIES. By WALTER BAGEHOT. 8vo., 10s. 6d.

Crump.—AN INVESTIGATION INTO THE CAUSES OF THE GREAT FALL IN PRICES which took place coincidently with the Demonetisation of Silver by Germany. By ARTHUR CRUMP. 8vo., 6s.

Devas.—A MANUAL OF POLITICAL ECONOMY. By C. S. DEVAS, M.A. Crown 8vo., 6s. 6d. (*Manuals of Catholic Philosophy.*)

Dowell.—A HISTORY OF TAXATION AND TAXES IN ENGLAND, from the Earliest Times to the Year 1885. By STEPHEN DOWELL. (4 vols. 8vo.) Vols. I. and II. The History of Taxation, 21s. Vols. III. and IV. The History of Taxes, 21s.

Jordan.—THE STANDARD OF VALUE. By WILLIAM LEIGHTON JORDAN. 8vo., 6s.

Leslie.—ESSAYS IN POLITICAL ECONOMY. By T. E. CLIFFE LESLIE. 8vo., 10s. 6d.

Macleod.—Works by HENRY DUNNING MACLEOD, M.A.

   THE ELEMENTS OF BANKING. Crown 8vo., 3s. 6d.

   THE THEORY AND PRACTICE OF BANKING. Vol. I. 8vo., 12s. Vol. II. 14s.

   THE THEORY OF CREDIT. 8vo. Vol. I. 10s. net. Vol. II., Part I., 4s. 6d. Vol. II. Part II., 10s. 6d.

Meath.—Works by The EARL OF MEATH.

   SOCIAL ARROWS: Reprinted Articles on various Social Subjects. Crown 8vo., 5s.

   PROSPERITY OR PAUPERISM? Physical, Industrial, and Technical Training. 8vo., 5s.

Mill.—POLITICAL ECONOMY. By JOHN STUART MILL.

   Silver Library Edition. Crown 8vo., 3s. 6d.

   Library Edition. 2 vols. 8vo., 30s.

Shirres.—AN ANALYSIS OF THE IDEAS OF ECONOMICS. By L. P. SHIRRES, B.A., sometime Finance Under Secretary of the Government of Bengal. Crown 8vo., 6s.

Political Economy and Economics—*continued.*

Symes.—POLITICAL ECONOMY: a Short Text-book of Political Economy. With Problems for Solution, and Hints for Supplementary Reading. By J. E. SYMES, M.A., of University College, Nottingham. Crown 8vo., 2*s.* 6*d.*

Toynbee.—LECTURES ON THE INDUSTRIAL REVOLUTION OF THE 18th CENTURY IN ENGLAND. By ARNOLD TOYNBEE. 8vo., 10*s.* 6*d.*

Wilson.—Works by A. J. WILSON. Chiefly reprinted from *The Investors' Review.*

PRACTICAL HINTS TO SMALL INVESTORS. Crown 8vo., 1*s.*

PLAIN ADVICE ABOUT LIFE INSURANCE. Crown 8vo., 1*s.*

Wolff.—PEOPLE'S BANKS: a Record of Social and Economic Success. By HENRY W. WOLFF. 8vo., 7*s.* 6*d.*

Evolution, Anthropology, &c.

Clodd.—THE STORY OF CREATION: a Plain Account of Evolution. By EDWARD CLODD. With 77 Illustrations. Crown 8vo., 3*s.* 6*d.*

Huth.—THE MARRIAGE OF NEAR KIN, considered with Respect to the Law of Nations, the Result of Experience, and the Teachings of Biology. By ALFRED HENRY HUTH. Royal 8vo., 21*s.*

Lang.—CUSTOM AND MYTH: Studies of Early Usage and Belief. By ANDREW LANG, M.A. With 15 Illustrations. Crown 8vo., 3*s.* 6*d.*

Lubbock.—THE ORIGIN OF CIVILISATION and the Primitive Condition of Man. By Sir J. LUBBOCK, Bart., M.P. With 5 Plates and 20 Illustrations in the Text. 8vo. 18*s.*

Romanes.—Works by GEORGE JOHN ROMANES, M.A., LL.D., F.R.S.

DARWIN, AND AFTER DARWIN: an Exposition of the Darwinian Theory, and a Discussion on Post-Darwinian Questions. Part I. The Darwinian Theory. With Portrait of Darwin and 125 Illustrations. Crown 8vo., 10*s.* 6*d.*

AN EXAMINATION OF WEISMANNISM. Crown 8vo., 6*s.*

Classical Literature.

Abbott.—HELLENICA. A Collection of Essays on Greek Poetry, Philosophy, History, and Religion. Edited by EVELYN ABBOTT, M.A., LL.D. 8vo., 16*s.*

Æschylus.—EUMENIDES OF ÆSCHYLUS. With Metrical English Translation. By J. F. DAVIES. 8vo., 7*s.*

Aristophanes.—The ACHARNIANS OF ARISTOPHANES, translated into English Verse. By R. Y. TYRRELL. Crown 8vo., 1*s.*

Becker.—Works by Professor BECKER.

GALLUS; or, Roman Scenes in the Time of Augustus. Illustrated. Post 8vo., 7*s.* 6*d.*

CHARICLES: or, Illustrations of the Private Life of the Ancient Greeks. Illustrated. Post 8vo., 7*s.* 6*d.*

Cicero.—CICERO'S CORRESPONDENCE. By R. Y. TYRRELL. Vols. I., II., III. 8vo., each 12*s.*

Clerke.—FAMILIAR STUDIES IN HOMER. By AGNES M. CLERKE. Cr. 8vo., 7*s.* 6*d.*

Farnell.—GREEK LYRIC POETRY: a Complete Collection of the Surviving Passages from the Greek Song-Writing. Arranged with Prefatory Articles, Introductory Matter and Commentary. By GEORGE S. FARNELL, M.A. With 5 Plates. 8vo., 16*s.*

Harrison.—MYTHS OF THE ODYSSEY. IN ART AND LITERATURE. By JANE E. HARRISON. Illustrated with Outline Drawings. 8vo., 18*s.*

Lang.—HOMER AND THE EPIC. By ANDREW LANG. Crown 8vo., 9*s.* net.

Classical Literature—*continued*.

Mackail.—SELECT EPIGRAMS FROM THE GREEK ANTHOLOGY. By J. W. MACKAIL, Fellow of Balliol College, Oxford. Edited with a Revised Text, Introduction, Translation, and Notes. 8vo., 16s.

Plato.—PARMENIDES OF PLATO, Text, with Introduction, Analysis, &c. By T. MAGUIRE. 8vo., 7s. 6d.

Rich.—A DICTIONARY OF ROMAN AND GREEK ANTIQUITIES. By A. RICH, B.A. With 2000 Woodcuts. Crown 8vo., 7s. 6d.

Sophocles.—Translated into English Verse. By ROBERT WHITELAW, M.A., Assistant Master in Rugby School: late Fellow of Trinity College, Cambridge. Crown 8vo., 8s. 6d.

Tyrrell.—TRANSLATIONS INTO GREEK AND LATIN VERSE. Edited by R. Y. TYRRELL. 8vo., 6s.

Virgil.—THE ÆNEID OF VIRGIL. Translated into English Verse by JOHN CONINGTON. Crown 8vo., 6s.

THE POEMS OF VIRGIL. Translated into English Prose by JOHN CONINGTON. Crown 8vo., 6s.

THE ÆNEID OF VIRGIL, freely translated into English Blank Verse. By W. J. THORNHILL. Crown 8vo., 7s. 6d.

THE ÆNEID OF VIRGIL. Books I. to VI. Translated into English Verse by JAMES RHOADES. Crown 8vo., 5s.

Wilkins.—THE GROWTH OF THE HOMERIC POEMS. By G. WILKINS. 8vo. 6s.

Poetry and the Drama.

Allingham.—Works by WILLIAM ALLINGHAM.

IRISH SONGS AND POEMS. With Frontispiece of the Waterfall of Asaroe. Fcp. 8vo., 6s.

LAURENCE BLOOMFIELD. With Portrait of the Author. Fcp. 8vo., 3s. 6d.

FLOWER PIECES; DAY AND NIGHT SONGS; BALLADS. With 2 Designs by D. G. ROSETTI. Fcp. 8vo., 6s.; large paper edition, 12s.

LIFE AND PHANTASY: with Frontispiece by Sir J. E. MILLAIS, Bart., and Design by ARTHUR HUGHES. Fcp. 8vo., 6s.; large paper edition, 12s.

THOUGHT AND WORD, AND ASHBY MANOR: a Play. With Portrait of the Author (1865), and four Theatrical Scenes drawn by Mr. Allingham. Fcp. 8vo., 6s.; large paper edition, 12s.

BLACKBERRIES. Imperial 16mo., 6s.

Sets of the above 6 vols. may be had in uniform half-parchment binding, price 30s.

Armstrong.—Works by G. F. SAVAGE-ARMSTRONG.

POEMS: Lyrical and Dramatic. Fcp. 8vo., 6s.

KING SAUL. (The Tragedy of Israel, Part I.) Fcp. 8vo. 5s.

KING DAVID. (The Tragedy of Israel, Part II.) Fcp. 8vo., 6s.

KING SOLOMON. (The Tragedy of Israel, Part III.) Fcp. 8vo., 6s.

UGONE: a Tragedy. Fcp. 8vo., 6s.

A GARLAND FROM GREECE: Poems. Fcp. 8vo., 7s. 6d.

STORIES OF WICKLOW: Poems. Fcp. 8vo., 7s. 6d.

MEPHISTOPHELES IN BROADCLOTH: a Satire. Fcp. 8vo., 4s.

ONE IN THE INFINITE: a Poem. Cr. 8vo., 7s. 6d.

Armstrong.—THE POETICAL WORKS OF EDMUND J. ARMSTRONG. Fcp. 8vo., 5s.

Poetry and the Drama—*continued*.

rnold.—Works by Sir EDWIN ARNOLD, K.C.I.E., Author of 'The Light of Asia,' &c.

THE LIGHT OF THE WORLD: or, the Great Consummation. A Poem. Crown 8vo., 7s. 6d. net.

Presentation Edition. With 14 Illustrations by W. HOLMAN HUNT, &c., 4to., 20s. net.

POTIPHAR'S WIFE, and other Poems. Crown 8vo., 5s. net.

ADZUMA : or, the Japanese Wife. A Play. Crown 8vo., 6s. 6d. net.

arrow.—THE SEVEN CITIES OF THE DEAD, and other Poems. By Sir JOHN CROKER BARROW, Bart. Fcp. 8vo., 5s.

ell.—Works by Mrs. HUGH BELL.

CHAMBER COMEDIES: a Collection of Plays and Monologues for the Drawing Room. Crown 8vo., 6s.

NURSERY COMEDIES: Twelve Tiny Plays for Children. Fcp. 8vo., 1s. 6d.

jörnsen.—PASTOR SANG: a Play. By BJÖRNSTJERNE BJÖRNSEN. Translated by WILLIAM WILSON. Cr. 8vo., 5s.

ante.—LA COMMEDIA DI DANTE. A New Text, carefully revised with the aid of the most recent Editions and Collations. Small 8vo., 6s.

oethe.

FAUST, Part I., the German Text, with Introduction and Notes. By ALBERT M. SELSS, Ph.D., M.A. Cr. 8vo., 5s.

FAUST. Translated, with Notes. By T. E. WEBB. 8vo., 12s. 6d.

FAUST. The First Part. A New Translation, chiefly in Blank Verse; with Introduction and Notes. By JAMES ADEY BIRDS. Cr. 8vo., 6s.

FAUST. The Second Part. A New Translation in Verse. By JAMES ADEY BIRDS. Crown 8vo., 6s.

Iaggard.—LIFE AND ITS AUTHOR: an Essay in Verse. By ELLA HAGGARD. With a Memoir by H. RIDER HAGGARD, and Portrait. Fcp. 8vo., 3s. 6d.

ngelow.—Works by JEAN INGELOW.

POETICAL WORKS. 2 vols. Fcp. 8vo., 12s.

LYRICAL AND OTHER POEMS. Selected from the Writings of JEAN INGELOW. Fcp. 8vo., 2s. 6d. cloth plain, 3s. cloth gilt.

Lang.—Works by ANDREW LANG.

GRASS OF PARNASSUS. Fcp. 8vo., 2s. 6d. net.

BALLADS OF BOOKS. Edited by ANDREW LANG. Fcp. 8vo., 6s.

THE BLUE POETRY BOOK. Edited by ANDREW LANG. With 12 Plates and 88 Illustrations in the Text. Crown 8vo., 6s.

Special Edition, printed on Indian paper. With Notes, but without Illustrations. Crown 8vo., 7s. 6d.

Lecky.—POEMS. By W. E. H. LECKY. Fcp. 8vo., 5s.

Leyton.—Works by FRANK LEYTON.

THE SHADOWS OF THE LAKE, and other Poems. Crown 8vo., 7s. 6d. Cheap Edition. Crown 8vo., 3s. 6d.

SKELETON LEAVES: Poems. Crown 8vo., 6s.

Longfellow.—THE HANGING OF THE CRANE, and other Poems of the Home. By HENRY W. LONGFELLOW. With Photogravure Illustrations. 16mo., 5s. 6d. net. [*Ready.*

Lytton.—Works by THE EARL OF LYTTON (OWEN MEREDITH).

MARAH. Fcp. 8vo., 6s. 6d.

KING POPPY: a Fantasia. With 1 Plate and Design on Title-Page by ED. BURNE-JONES, A.R.A. Crown 8vo., 10s. 6d.

THE WANDERER. Cr. 8vo., 10s. 6d.

Macaulay.—LAYS OF ANCIENT ROME, &c. By Lord MACAULAY.

Illustrated by G. SCHARF. Fcp. 4to., 10s. 6d.

———— Bijou Edition. 18mo., 2s. 6d., gilt top.

———— Popular Edition. Fcp. 4to., 6d. sewed, 1s. cloth.

Illustrated by J. R. WEGUELIN. Crown 8vo., 3s. 6d.

Annotated Edition. Fcp. 8vo., 1s. sewed, 1s. 6d. cloth.

Nesbit.—LAYS AND LEGENDS. by E. NESBIT (Mrs. HUBERT BLAND). First Series. Crown 8vo., 3s. 6d. Second Series, with Portrait. Crown 8vo., 5s.

Piatt.—AN ENCHANTED CASTLE, AND OTHER POEMS: Pictures, Portraits and People in Ireland. By SARAH PIATT. Crown 8vo., 3s. 6d.

Poetry and the Drama—*continu[ed]*

Piatt.—Works by JOHN JAMES PIATT.

   IDYLS AND LYRICS OF THE OHIO VALLEY. Crown 8vo., 5s.

   LITTLE NEW WORLD IDYLS. Cr. 8vo., 5s.

Rhoades.—TERESA AND OTHER POEMS. By JAMES RHOADES. Crown 8vo., 3s. 6d.

Riley.—Works by JAMES WHITCOMB RILEY.

   POEMS HERE AT HOME. Fcap. 8vo., 6s. net.

   OLD FASHIONED ROSES: Poems. 12mo., 5s.

Roberts.—SONGS OF THE COMMON DAY, AND AVE: an Ode for the Shelley Centenary. By CHARLES G. D. ROBERTS. Crown 8vo., 3s. 6d.

Shakespeare.—SHAKESPEARE. 1 vol. 8vo., 14[s] 8vo., 21s.

   THE SHAKESPE[ARE] By MARY F. L[ ] Drawing-Roo[m] graphs. Fcp.

Stevenson.—A[ ] VERSES. By R[ ] SON. Small fcp.

Whittier.—Wo[rks] LEAF WHITTIER[ ]

   SNOW-BOUND: 10 Photograv[ures] H. GARRETT.

   AT SUNDOWN: [por]trait and 8 [ ] GARRETT. C[ ]

Works of Fiction, Humour, [&c.]

Anstey.—Works by F. ANSTEY, Author of 'Vice Versâ'.

   THE BLACK POODLE, and other Stories. Crown 8vo., 2s. boards, 2s. 6d. cloth.

   VOCES POPULI. Reprinted from 'Punch'. With Illustrations by J. BERNARD PARTRIDGE. First Series. Fcp. 4to., 5s. Second Series. Fcp. 4to., 6s.

   THE TRAVELLING COMPANIONS. Reprinted from 'Punch'. With Illustrations by J. BERNARD PARTRIDGE. Post 4to., 5s.

   THE MAN FROM BLANKLEY'S: a Story in Scenes, and other Sketches. With 24 Illustrations by J. BERNARD PARTRIDGE. Fcp. 4to., 6s.

ATELIER (THE) DU LYS: or, an Art Student in the Reign of Terror. Crown 8vo., 2s. 6d.

   BY THE SAME AUTHOR.

   MADEMOISELLE MORI: a Tale of Modern Rome. Crown 8vo., 2s. 6d.

BY THE SAME A[UTHOR.]

   THAT CHILD. [ ] BROWNE. Cr[ ]

   UNDER A CLOU[D]

   THE FIDDLER O[F] trations by W[ ] 8vo., 2s. 6d.

   A CHILD OF THE[ ] Illustrations b[y] Crown 8vo., 2s[ ]

   HESTER'S VENT[URE] 8vo., 2s. 6d.

   IN THE OLDEN [ ] Peasant War[ ] 8vo., 2s. 6d.

   THE YOUNGER [ ] 8vo., 6s.

Baker.—BY THE[ ] JAMES BAKER, A[ ] cott'. Crown 8v[o.]

Works of Fiction, Humour, &c.—*continued.*

Beaconsfield.—Works by the Earl of BEACONSFIELD.
NOVELS AND TALES. Cheap Edition. Complete in 11 vols. Cr. 8vo., 1s. 6d. each.
Vivian Grey. | Contarini Fleming, &c.
The Young Duke, &c. | Venetia. Tancred.
Alroy, Ixion, &c. | Coningsby. Sybil.
Henrietta Temple. | Lothair. Endymion.
NOVELS AND TALES. The Hughenden Edition. With 2 Portraits and 11 Vignettes. 11 vols. Cr. 8vo., 42s.

Comyn.—ATHERSTONE PRIORY: a Tale. By L. N. COMYN. Crown 8vo., 2s. 6d.

Deland.—Works by MARGARET DELAND, Author of 'John Ward'.
THE STORY OF A CHILD. Cr. 8vo., 5s.
MR TOMMY DOVE, and other Stories. Crown 8vo., 6s.

Dougall.—Works by L. DOUGALL.
BEGGARS ALL. Crown 8vo., 3s. 6d.
WHAT NECESSITY KNOWS. 3 vols. Crown 8vo., £1 5s. 6d.

Doyle.—Works by A. CONAN DOYLE.
MICAH CLARKE: a Tale of Monmouth's Rebellion. With Frontispiece and Vignette. Cr. 8vo., 3s. 6d.
THE CAPTAIN OF THE POLESTAR, and other Tales. Cr. 8vo., 3s. 6d.
THE REFUGEES: a Tale of Two Continents. Cr. 8vo., 6s.

Farrar.—DARKNESS AND DAWN: or, Scenes in the Days of Nero. An Historic Tale. By Archdeacon FARRAR. Cr. 8vo., 7s. 6d.

Froude.—THE TWO CHIEFS OF DUNBOY: an Irish Romance of the Last Century. By J. A. FROUDE. Cr. 8vo., 3s. 6d.

Haggard.—Works by H. RIDER HAGGARD.
SHE. With 32 Illustrations by M. GREIFFENHAGEN and C. H. M. KERR. Cr. 8vo., 3s. 6d.
ALLAN QUATERMAIN. With 31 Illustrations by C. H. M. KERR. Cr. 8vo., 3s. 6d.
MAIWA'S REVENGE; or, The War of the Little Hand. Cr. 8vo., 1s. 6d. boards, 1s. 6d. cloth.
COLONEL QUARITCH, V.C. Cr. 8vo., 3s. 6d.

Haggard.—Works by H. RIDER HAGGARD—*continued.*
CLEOPATRA. With 29 Full-page Illustrations by M. GREIFFENHAGEN and R. CATON WOODVILLE. Cr. 8vo., 3s. 6d.
BEATRICE. Cr. 8vo., 3s. 6d.
ERIC BRIGHTEYES. With 17 Plates and 34 Illustrations in the Text by LANCELOT SPEED. Cr. 8vo., 3s. 6d.
NADA THE LILY. With 23 Illustrations by C. H. M. KERR. Cr. 8vo., 6s.
MONTEZUMA'S DAUGHTER. With Illustrations by M. GREIFFENHAGEN. Cr. 8vo., 6s.

Haggard and Lang.—THE WORLD'S DESIRE. By H. RIDER HAGGARD and ANDREW LANG. Cr. 8vo., 6s.

Harte.—IN THE CARQUINEZ WOODS, and other Stories. By BRET HARTE. Cr. 8vo., 3s. 6d.

KEITH DERAMORE: a Novel. By the Author of 'Miss Molly'. Cr. 8vo., 6s.

Lyall.—THE AUTOBIOGRAPHY OF A SLANDER. By EDNA LYALL, Author of 'Donovan,' &c. Fcp. 8vo., 1s. sewed.
Presentation Edition. With 20 Illustrations by LANCELOT SPEED. Cr. 8vo., 5s.

Melville.—Works by G. J. WHYTE MELVILLE.
The Gladiators. | Holmby House.
The Interpreter. | Kate Coventry.
Good for Nothing. | Digby Grand.
The Queen's Maries. | General Bounce.
Cr. 8vo., 1s. 6d. each.

Oliphant.—Works by Mrs. OLIPHANT.
MADAM. Cr. 8vo., 1s. 6d.
IN TRUST. Cr. 8vo., 1s. 6d.

Parr.—CAN THIS BE LOVE? By Mrs. PARR, Author of 'Dorothy Fox'. Cr. 8vo., 6s.

Payn.—Works by JAMES PAYN.
THE LUCK OF THE DARRELLS. Cr. 8vo., 1s. 6d.
THICKER THAN WATER. Cr. 8vo., 1s. 6d.

Phillipps-Wolley.—SNAP: a Legend of the Lone Mountain. By C. PHILLIPPS-WOLLEY. With 13 Illustrations by H. G. WILLINK. Cr. 8vo., 3s. 6d.

Robertson.—THE KIDNAPPED SQUATTER, and other Australian Tales. By A. ROBERTSON. Cr. 8vo., 6s.

Works of Fiction, Humour, &c.—continued.

Sewell.—Works by ELIZABETH M. SEWELL.
A Glimpse of the World. | Amy Herbert.
Laneton Parsonage. | Cleve Hall.
Margaret Percival. | Gertrude.
Katharine Ashton. | Home Life.
The Earl's Daughter. | After Life.
The Experience of Life. | Ursula. Ivors.
Cr. 8vo., 1s. 6d. each cloth plain. 2s. 6d. each cloth extra, gilt edges.

Stevenson.—Works by ROBERT LOUIS STEVENSON.
STRANGE CASE OF DR. JEKYLL AND MR. HYDE. Fcp. 8vo., 1s. sewed. 1s. 6d. cloth.
THE DYNAMITER. Fcp. 8vo., 1s. sewed, 1s. 6d. cloth.

Stevenson and Osbourne.—THE WRONG BOX. By ROBERT LOUIS STEVENSON and LLOYD OSBOURNE. Cr. 8vo., 3s. 6d.

Sturgis.—AFTER TWENTY YEARS, and other Stories. By JULIAN STURGIS. Cr. 8vo., 6s.

Suttner.—LAY DOWN YOUR ARMS Die Waffen Nieder: The Autobiography of Martha Tilling. By BERTHA VON STUTTNER. Translated by T. HOLMES. Cr. 8vo., 7s. 6d.

Thompson.—A MORAL DILEMMA: Novel. By ANNIE THOMPSON. Cr 8vo., 6s.

Tirebuck.—Works by WILLIAM TIRE BUCK.
DORRIE. Crown 8vo., 6s.
SWEETHEART GWEN. Cr. 8vo., 6s.

Trollope.—Works by ANTHONY TROLLOPE.
THE WARDEN. Cr. 8vo., 1s. 6d.
BARCHESTER TOWERS. Cr. 8vo., 1s. 6d

Walford.—Works by L. B. WALFORD Author of 'Mr. Smith'.
THE MISCHIEF OF MONICA: a Novel Cr. 8vo., 2s. 6d.
THE ONE GOOD GUEST: a Story. Cr 8vo, 6s.

West.—HALF-HOURS WITH THE MILLIONAIRES; Showing how much harde it is to spend a million than to make it Edited by B. B. WEST. Cr. 8vo., 6s.

Weyman.—Works by STANLEY J WEYMAN.
THE HOUSE OF THE WOLF: a Romance Cr. 8vo., 3s. 6d.
A GENTLEMAN OF FRANCE.. 3 vols Cr. 8vo.

Popular Science (Natural History, &c.).

Butler.—OUR HOUSEHOLD INSECTS. By E. A. BUTLER. With 7 Plates and 113 Illustrations in the Text. Crown 8vo., 6s.

Furneaux.—THE OUTDOOR WORLD; or, The Young Collector's Handbook. By W. FURNEAUX, F.R.G.S. With 16 Coloured Plates, 2 Plain Plates, and 549 Illustrations in the Text. Crown 8vo., 7s. 6d.

Hartwig.—Works by Dr. GEORGE HARTWIG.
THE SEA AND ITS LIVING WONDERS. With 12 Plates and 303 Woodcuts. 8vo., 7s. net.
THE TROPICAL WORLD. With 8 Plates and 172 Woodcuts. 8vo., 7s. net.
THE POLAR WORLD. With 3 Maps, 8 Plates and 85 Woodcuts. 8vo., 7s. net.

Hartwig.—Works by Dr. GEORGE HARTWIG—continued.
THE SUBTERRANEAN WORLD. With 3 Maps and 80 Woodcuts. 8vo., 7. net.
THE AERIAL WORLD. With Map, Plates and 60 Woodcuts. 8vo., 7. net.
HEROES OF THE POLAR WORLD. 1 Illustrations. Crown 8vo., 2s.
WONDERS OF THE TROPICAL FORESTS 40 Illustrations. Crown 8vo., 2s.
WORKERS UNDER THE GROUND. 2 Illustrations. Crown 8vo., 2s.
MARVELS OVER OUR HEADS. 29 I lustrations. Crown 8vo., 2s.
SEA MONSTERS AND SEA BIRDS. 7 Illustrations. Crown 8vo., 2s. 6d.

Popular Science (Natural History, &c.).

Hartwig.—Works by Dr. George Hartwig—*continued*.

DENIZENS OF THE DEEP. 117 Illustrations. Crown 8vo., 2s. 6d.

VOLCANOES AND EARTHQUAKES. 30 Illustrations. Crown 8vo., 2s. 6d.

WILD ANIMALS OF THE TROPICS. 66 Illustrations. Crown 8vo., 3s. 6d.

Helmholtz.—POPULAR LECTURES ON SCIENTIFIC SUBJECTS. By Professor HELMHOLTZ. With 68 Woodcuts. 2 vols. Crown 8vo., 3s. 6d. each.

Lydekker.—PHASES OF ANIMAL LIFE, PAST AND PRESENT. By R. LYDEKKER, B.A. With 82 Illustrations. Crown 8vo., 6s.

Proctor.—Works by RICHARD A. PROCTOR.

And see Messrs. Longmans & Co.'s Catalogue of Scientific Works.

LIGHT SCIENCE FOR LEISURE HOURS. Familiar Essays on Scientific Subjects. 3 vols. Crown 8vo., 5s. each.

CHANCE AND LUCK: a Discussion of the Laws of Luck, Coincidence, Wagers, Lotteries and the Fallacies of Gambling, &c. Cr. 8vo., 2s. boards, 2s. 6d. cloth.

ROUGH WAYS MADE SMOOTH. Familiar Essays on Scientific Subjects. Crown 8vo., 5s. Silver Library Edition. Crown 8vo., 3s. 6d.

PLEASANT WAYS IN SCIENCE. Cr. 8vo., 5s. Silver Library Edition. Crown 8vo., 3s. 6d.

THE GREAT PYRAMID, OBSERVATORY, TOMB AND TEMPLE. With Illustrations. Crown 8vo., 5s.

NATURE STUDIES. By R. A. PROCTOR, GRANT ALLEN, A. WILSON, T. FOSTER and E. CLODD. Crown 8vo., 5s. Silver Library Edition. Crown 8vo., 3s. 6d.

LEISURE READINGS. By R. A. PROCTOR, E. CLODD, A. WILSON, T. FOSTER, and A. C. RANYARD. Cr. 8vo., 5s.

Stanley.—A FAMILIAR HISTORY OF BIRDS. By E. STANLEY, D.D., formerly Bishop of Norwich. With Illustrations. Cr. 8vo., 3s. 6d.

Wood.—Works by the Rev. J. G. WOOD.

HOMES WITHOUT HANDS: a Description of the Habitation of Animals, classed according to the Principle of Construction. With 140 Illustrations. 8vo., 7s. net.

INSECTS AT HOME: a Popular Account of British Insects, their Structure, Habits and Transformations. With 700 Illustrations. 8vo., 7s. net.

INSECTS ABROAD: a Popular Account of Foreign Insects, their Structure, Habits and Transformations. With 600 Illustrations. 8vo., 7s. net.

BIBLE ANIMALS: a Description of every Living Creature mentioned in the Scriptures. With 112 Illustrations. 8vo., 7s. net.

PETLAND REVISITED. With 33 Illustrations. Cr. 8vo., 3s. 6d.

OUT OF DOORS; a Selection of Original Articles on Practical Natural History. With 11 Illustrations. Cr. 8vo., 3s. 6d.

STRANGE DWELLINGS: a Description of the Habitations of Animals, abridged from 'Homes without Hands'. With 60 Illustrations. Cr. 8vo., 3s. 6d.

BIRD LIFE OF THE BIBLE. 32 Illustrations. Cr. 8vo., 3s. 6d.

WONDERFUL NESTS. 30 Illustrations. Cr. 8vo., 3s. 6d.

HOMES UNDER THE GROUND. 28 Illustrations. Cr. 8vo., 3s. 6d.

WILD ANIMALS OF THE BIBLE. 29 Illustrations. Cr. 8vo., 3s. 6d.

DOMESTIC ANIMALS OF THE BIBLE. 23 Illustrations. Cr. 8vo., 3s. 6d.

THE BRANCH BUILDERS. 28 Illustrations. Cr. 8vo., 2s. 6d.

SOCIAL HABITATIONS AND PARASITIC NESTS. 18 Illustrations. Cr. 8vo., 2s.

Works of Reference.

Maunder's (Samuel) Treasuries.

BIOGRAPHICAL TREASURY. With Supplement brought down to 1889. By Rev. JAMES WOOD. Fcp. 8vo., 6s.

TREASURY OF NATURAL HISTORY: or, Popular Dictionary of Zoology. With 900 Woodcuts. Fcp. 8vo., 6s.

TREASURY OF GEOGRAPHY, Physical, Historical, Descriptive, and Political. With 7 Maps and 16 Plates. Fcp. 8vo., 6s.

THE TREASURY OF BIBLE KNOWLEDGE. By the Rev. J. AYRE, M.A. With 5 Maps, 15 plates, and 300 Woodcuts. Fcp. 8vo., 6s.

HISTORICAL TREASURY: Outlines of Universal History, Separate Histories of all Nations. Fcp. 8vo., 6s.

TREASURY OF KNOWLEDGE AND LIBRARY OF REFERENCE. Comprising an English Dictionary and Grammar, Universal Gazeteer, Classical Dictionary, Chronology, Law Dictionary, &c. Fcp. 8vo., 6s.

Maunder's (Samuel) Treasuries —*continued.*

SCIENTIFIC AND LITERARY TREASURY. Fcp. 8vo., 6s.

THE TREASURY OF BOTANY. Edited by J. LINDLEY, F.R.S., and T. MOORE, F.L.S. With 274 Woodcuts and 20 Steel Plates. 2 vols. Fcp. 8vo., 12s.

Roget.—THESAURUS OF ENGLISH WORDS AND PHRASES. Classified and Arranged so as to Faciltiate the Expression of Ideas and assist in Literary Composition. By PETER MARK ROGET, M.D., F.R.S. Recomposed throughout, enlarged and improved, partly from the Author's Notes, and with a full Index, by the Author's Son, JOHN LEWIS ROGET. Crown 8vo., 10s. 6d.

Willich.—POPULAR TABLES for giving information for ascertaining the value of Lifehold, Leasehold, and Church Property, the Public Funds, &c. By CHARLES M. WILLICH. Edited by H. BENCE JONES. Crown 8vo., 10s. 6d.

Children's Books.

Crake.—Works by Rev. A. D. CRAKE.

EDWY THE FAIR; or, the First Chronicle of Æscendune. Crown 8vo., 2s. 6d.

ALFGAR THE DANE: or, the Second Chronicle of Æscendune. Cr. 8vo., 2s. 6d.

THE RIVAL HEIRS: being the Third and Last Chronicle of Æscendune. Cr. 8vo., 2s. 6d.

THE HOUSE OF WALDERNE. A Tale of the Cloister and the Forest in the Days of the Barons' Wars. Crown 8vo., 2s. 6d.

BRIAN FITZ-COUNT. A Story of Wallingford Castle and Dorchester Abbey. Cr. 8vo., 2s. 6d.

Lang.—Works edited by ANDREW LANG.

THE BLUE FAIRY BOOK. With 8 Plates and 130 Illustrations in the Text by H. J. FORD and G. P. JACOMB HOOD. Crown 8vo., 6s.

Lang.—Works edited by ANDREW LANG —*continued.*

THE RED FAIRY BOOK. With 4 Plates and 96 Illustrations in the Text by H. J. FORD and LANCELOT SPEED. Crown 8vo., 6s.

THE GREEN FAIRY BOOK. With 11 Plates and 88 Illustrations in the Text by H. J. FORD and L. BOGLE. Cr. 8vo., 6s.

THE BLUE POETRY BOOK. With 12 Plates and 88 Illustration in the Text by H. J. FORD and LANCELOT SPEED. Crown 8vo., 6s.

THE BLUE POETRY BOOK. School Edition, without Illustrations. Fcp. 8vo., 2s. 6d.

THE TRUE STORY BOOK. With 8 Plates and 58 Illustrations in the Text, by C. H. KERR, H. J. FORD, LANCELOT SPEED, and L. BOGLE. Crown 8vo., 6s.

Children's Books—*continued.*

Meade.—Works by L. T. MEADE.
DEB AND THE DUCHESS. Illustrated. Crown 8vo., 3s. 6d.
THE BERESFORD PRIZE. Illustrated. Cr. 8vo., 5s.
DADDY'S BOY. Illustrated. Crown 8vo., 3s. 6d.

Molesworth.—Works by Mrs. MOLESWORTH.
SILVERTHORNS. Illustrated. Cr. 8vo., 5s.
THE PALACE IN THE GARDEN. Illustrated. Crown 8vo., 5s.
THE THIRD MISS ST. QUENTIN. Cr. 8vo., 6s.
NEIGHBOURS. Illustrated. Cr. 8vo., 6s.
THE STORY OF A SPRING MORNING, &c. Illustrated. Crown 8vo., 5s.

Reader.— VOICES FROM FLOWERLAND: a Birthday Book and Language of Flowers. By EMILY E. READER. Illustrated by ADA BROOKE. Royal 16mo., cloth, 2s. 6d.; vegetable vellum, 3s. 6d.

Stevenson.—Works by ROBERT LOUIS STEVENSON.
A CHILD'S GARDEN OF VERSES. Small fcp. 8vo., 5s.
A CHILD'S GARLAND OF SONGS, Gathered from 'A Child's Garden of Verses'. Set to Music by C. VILLIERS STANFORD, Mus. Doc. 4to., 2s. sewed; 3s. 6d., cloth gilt.

The Silver Library.

CROWN 8vo. 3s. 6d. EACH VOLUME.

Baker's (Sir S. W.) Eight Years in Ceylon. With 6 Illustrations. 3s. 6d.
Baker's (Sir S. W.) Rifle and Hound in Ceylon. With 6 Illustrations. 3s. 6d.
Baring-Gould's (Rev. S.) Curious Myths of the Middle Ages. 3s. 6d.
Baring-Gould's (Rev. S.) Origin and Development of Religious Belief. 2 vols. 3s. 6d. each.
Brassey's (Lady) A Voyage in the 'Sunbeam'. With 66 Illustrations. 3s. 6d.
Clodd's (E.) Story of Creation: a Plain Account of Evolution. With 77 Illustrations. 3s. 6d.
Conybeare (Rev. W. J.) and Howson's (Very Rev. J. S.) Life and Epistles of St. Paul. 46 Illustrations. 3s. 6d.
Dougall's (L.) Beggars All; a Novel. 3s. 6d.
Doyle's (A. Conan) Micah Clarke: a Tale of Monmouth's Rebellion. 3s. 6d.
Doyle's (A. Conan) The Captain of the Polestar, and other Tales. 3s. 6d.
Froude's (J. A.) Short Studies on Great Subjects. 4 vols. 3s. 6d. each.
Froude's (J. A.) Cæsar: a Sketch. 3s. 6d.
Froude's (J. A.) Thomas Carlyle: a History of his Life.
1795-1835. 2 vols. 7s.
1834-1881. 2 vols. 7s.
Froude's (J. A.) The Two Chiefs of Dunboy. 3s. 6d.
Froude's (J. A.) The History of England, from the Fall of Wolsey to the Defeat of the Spanish Armada. 12 vols. 3s. 6d. each.

Gleig's (Rev. G. R.) Life of the Duke of Wellington. With Portrait. 3s. 6d.
Haggard's (H. R.) She: A History of Adventure. 32 Illustrations. 3s. 6d.
Haggard's (H. R.) Allan Quatermain. With 20 Illustrations. 3s. 6d.
Haggard's (H. R.) Colonel Quaritch, V.C.: a Tale of Country Life. 3s. 6d.
Haggard's (H. R.) Cleopatra. With 29 Full-page Illustrations. 3s. 6d.
Haggard's (H. R.) Eric Brighteyes. With 51 Illustrations. 3s. 6d.
Haggard's (H. R.) Beatrice. 3s. 6d.
Harte's (Bret) In the Carquinez Woods, and other Stories. 3s. 6d.
Helmholtz's (Professor) Popular Lectures on Scientific Subjects. With 68 Woodcuts. 2 vols. 3s. 6d. each.
Howitt's (W.) Visits to Remarkable Places. 80 Illustrations. 3s. 6d.
Jefferies' (R.) The Story of My Heart: My Autobiography. With Portrait. 3s. 6d.
Jefferies' (R.) Field and Hedgerow. With Portrait. 3s. 6d.
Jefferies' (R.) Red Deer. With 17 Illustrations. 3s. 6d.
Jefferies' (R.) Wood Magic: a Fable. 3s. 6d.
Knight's (E. F.) The Cruise of the 'Alerte': the Narrative of a Search for Treasure on the Desert Island of Trinidad. With 2 Maps and 23 Illustrations. 3s. 6d.

The Silver Library—*continued.*

Lang's (A.) Custom and Myth: Studies of Early Usage and Belief. 3s. 6d.

Lees (J. A.) and Clutterbuck's (W. J.) B.C. 1887, A Ramble in British Columbia. With Maps and 75 Illustrations. 3s. 6d.

Macaulay's (Lord) Essays and Lays of Ancient Rome. With Portrait and Illustrations. 3s. 6d.

Macleod (H. D.) The Elements of Banking. 3s. 6d.

Marshman's (J. C.) Memoirs of Sir Henry Havelock. 3s. 6d.

Max Müller's (F.) India, what can it teach us? 3s. 6d.

Max Müller's (F.) Introduction to the Science of Religion. 3s. 6d.

Merivale's (Dean) History of the Romans under the Empire. 8 vols. 3s. 6d. ea.

Mill's (J. S.) Political Economy. 3s. 6d.

Mill's (J. S.) System of Logic. 3s. 6d.

Milner's (Geo.) Country Pleasures: the Chronicle of a Year chiefly in a Garden. 3s. 6d.

Newman's (Cardinal) Apologia Pro Vita Sua. 3s. 6d.

Newman's (Cardinal) Historical Sketches. 3 vols. 3s. 6d. each.

Newman's (Cardinal) Callista: a Tale of the Third Century. 3s. 6d.

Newman's (Cardinal) Loss and Gain: a Tale. 3s. 6d.

Newman's (Cardinal) Essays, Critical and Historical. 2 vols. 7s.

Newman's (Cardinal) An Essay on the Development of Christian Doctrine. 3s. 6d.

Newman's (Cardinal) The Arians of the Fourth Century. 3s. 6d.

Newman's (Cardinal) Verses on Various Occasions. 3s. 6d.

Newman's (Cardinal) The Present Position of Catholics in England. 3s. 6d.

Newman's (Cardinal) Parochial and Plain Sermons. 8 vols. 3s. 6d. each.

Newman's (Cardinal) Selection, adapted to the Seasons of the Ecclesiastical Year, from the 'Parochial and Plain Sermons'. 3s. 6d.

Newman's (Cardinal) Sermons bearing upon Subjects of the Day. 3s. 6d.

Newman's (Cardinal) Difficulties felt by Anglicans in Catholic Teaching Considered. 2 vols. 3s. 6d. each.

Newman's (Cardinal) The Idea of University. 3s. 6d.

Newman's (Cardinal) Biblical and Ecclesiastical Miracles. 3s. 6d.

Newman's (Cardinal) Discussions and Arguments. 3s. 6d.

Newman's (Cardinal) Grammar of Assent. 3s. 6d.

Newman's (Cardinal) Fifteen Sermons Preached before the University of Oxford. 3s. 6d.

Newman's (Cardinal) Lectures on the Doctrine of Justification. 3s. 6d.

Newman's (Cardinal) Sermons on Various Occasions. 3s. 6d.

Newman's (Cardinal) The Via Media of the Anglican Church, illustrated in Lectures, &c. 2 vols. 3s. 6d. each.

Newman's (Cardinal) Discourses to Mixed Congregations. 3s. 6d.

Phillipps-Wolley's (C.) Snap: a Legend of the Lone Mountain. With Illustrations. 3s. 6d.

Proctor's (R. A.) Other Worlds than Ours. 3s. 6d.

Proctor's (R. A.) Rough Ways made Smooth. 3s. 6d.

Proctor's (R. A.) Pleasant Ways in Science. 3s. 6d.

Proctor's (R. A.) Myths and Marvels of Astronomy. 3s. 6d.

Proctor's (R. A.) Nature Studies. 3s. 6d.

Stanley's (Bishop) Familiar History of Birds. 160 Illustrations. 3s. 6d.

Stevenson (Robert Louis) and Osbourne's (Lloyd) The Wrong Box. 3s. 6d.

Weyman's (Stanley J.) The House of the Wolf: a Romance. 3s. 6d.

Wood's (Rev. J. G.) Petland Revisited. With 33 Illustrations. 3s. 6d.

Wood's (Rev. J. G.) Strange Dwellings. With 60 Illustrations. 3s. 6d.

Wood's (Rev. J. G.) Out of Doors. Illustrations. 3s. 6d.

Cookery, Domestic Management, &c.

Acton.—MODERN COOKERY. By ELIZA ACTON. With 150 Woodcuts. Fcp. 8vo., 4s. 6d.

Bull.—Works by THOMAS BULL, M.D.

HINTS TO MOTHERS ON THE MANAGEMENT OF THEIR HEALTH DURING THE PERIOD OF PREGNANCY. Fcp. 8vo., 1s. 6d.

THE MATERNAL MANAGEMENT OF CHILDREN IN HEALTH AND DISEASE. Fcp. 8vo., 1s. 6d.

Cookery, Domestic Management, &c.—*continued*.

De Salis.—Works by Mrs. DE SALIS.
CAKES AND CONFECTIONS À LA MODE. Fcp. 8vo., 1s. 6d.
DOGS: a Manual for Amateurs. Fcp. 8vo., 1s. 6d.
DRESSED GAME AND POULTRY À LA MODE. Fcp. 8vo., 1s. 6d.
DRESSED VEGETABLES À LA MODE. Fcp. 8vo., 1s. 6d.
DRINKS À LA MODE. Fcp. 8vo., 1s. 6d.
ENTRÉES À LA MODE. Fcp. 8vo., 1s. 6d.
OYSTERS À LA MODE. Fcp. 8vo., 1s. 6d.
PUDDINGS AND PASTRY À LA MODE. Fcp. 8vo., 1s. 6d.
SAVOURIES À LA MODE. Fcp. 8vo., 1s. 6d.
SOUPS AND DRESSED FISH À LA MODE. Fcp. 8vo., 1s. 6d.
SWEETS AND SUPPER DISHES À LA MODE. Fcp. 8vo., 1s. 6d.
TEMPTING DISHES FOR SMALL INCOMES. Fcp. 8vo., 1s. 6d.

De Salis.—Works by Mrs. DE SALIS—*continued*.
FLORAL DECORATIONS. Suggestions and Descriptions. Fcp. 8vo., 1s. 6d.
NEW-LAID EGGS: Hints for Amateur Poultry Rearers. Fcp. 8vo., 1s. 6d.
WRINKLES AND NOTIONS FOR EVERY HOUSEHOLD. Cr. 8vo., 1s. 6d.

Harrison.—COOKERY FOR BUSY LIVES AND SMALL INCOMES. By MARY HARRISON. Cr. 8vo., 1s.

Lear.—MAIGRE COOKERY. By H. L. SIDNEY LEAR. 16mo., 2s.

Poole.—COOKERY FOR THE DIABETIC. By W. H. and Mrs. POOLE. With Preface by Dr. PAVY. Fcp. 8vo., 2s. 6d.

Walker.—A HANDBOOK FOR MOTHERS: being Simple Hints to Women on the Management of their Health during Pregnancy and Confinement, together with Plain Directions as to the Care of Infants. By JANE H. WALKER, L.R.C.P. and L.M. L.R.C.S. and M.D. (Brux.). With 13 Illustrations. Cr. 8vo., 2s. 6d.

Miscellaneous and Critical Works.

Armstrong.—ESSAYS AND SKETCHES. By EDMUND J. ARMSTRONG. Fcp. 8vo., 5s.

Bagehot.—LITERARY STUDIES. By WALTER BAGEHOT. 2 vols. 8vo., 28s.

Baring-Gould.—CURIOUS MYTHS OF THE MIDDLE AGES. By Rev. S. BARING-GOULD. Crown 8vo., 3s. 6d.

Boyd ('A. K. H. B.').—Works by A. K. H. BOYD, D.D.
AUTUMN HOLIDAYS OF A COUNTRY PARSON. Crown 8vo., 3s. 6d.
COMMONPLACE PHILOSOPHER. Crown 8vo., 3s. 6d.
CRITICAL ESSAYS OF A COUNTRY PARSON. Crown 8vo., 3s. 6d.
EAST COAST DAYS AND MEMORIES. Crown 8vo., 3s. 6d.
LANDSCAPES, CHURCHES AND MORALITIES. Crown 8vo., 3s. 6d.
LEISURE HOURS IN TOWN. Crown 8vo., 3s. 6d.
LESSONS OF MIDDLE AGE. Crown 8vo., 3s. 6d.
OUR LITTLE LIFE. Two Series. Cr. 8vo., 3s. 6d. each.
OUR HOMELY COMEDY: AND TRAGEDY. Crown 8vo., 3s. 6d.
RECREATIONS OF A COUNTRY PARSON. Three Series. Cr. 8vo., 3s. 6d. each. First Series. Popular Ed. 8vo., 6d. swd.

Butler.—Works by SAMUEL BUTLER.
Op. 1. EREWHON. Cr. 8vo., 5s.
Op. 2. THE FAIR HAVEN. A Work in Defence of the Miraculous Element in our Lord's Ministry. Cr. 8vo., 7s. 6d.
Op. 3. LIFE AND HABIT. An Essay after a Completer View of Evolution. Cr. 8vo., 7s. 6d.
Op. 4. EVOLUTION, OLD AND NEW. Cr. 8vo., 10s. 6d.
Op. 5. UNCONSCIOUS MEMORY. Cr. 8vo., 7s. 6d.
Op. 6. ALPS AND SANCTUARIES OF PIEDMONT AND CANTON TICINO. Illustrated. Post 4to., 10s. 6d.
Op. 7. SELECTIONS FROM OPS. 1-6. With Remarks on Mr. ROMANES' 'Mental Evolution in Animals'. Cr. 8vo., 7s. 6d.
Op. 8. LUCK, OR CUNNING, AS THE MAIN MEANS OF ORGANIC MODIFICATION? Cr. 8vo., 7s. 6d.
Op. 9. EX VOTO. An Account of the Sacro Monte or New Jerusalem at Varallo-Sesioa. 10s. 6d.
HOLBEIN'S 'LA DANSE'. A Note on a Drawing called 'La Danse'. 3s.

Miscellaneous and Critical Works—*continued.*

Halliwell-Phillipps.—A CALENDAR OF THE HALLIWELL-PHILLIPPS COLLECTION OF SHAKESPEAREAN RARITIES. Enlarged by ERNEST E. BAKER, F.S.A. 8vo., 10s. 6d.

Hodgson.—OUTCAST ESSAYS AND VERSE TRANSLATIONS. By W. SHADWORTH HODGSON. Crown 8vo., 8s. 6d.

Hullah.—Works by JOHN HULLAH, LL.D.
  COURSE OF LECTURES ON THE HISTORY OF MODERN MUSIC. 8vo., 8s. 6d.
  COURSE OF LECTURES ON THE TRANSITION PERIOD OF MUSICAL HISTORY. 8vo., 10s. 6d.

Jefferies.—Works by RICHARD JEFFERIES.
  FIELD AND HEDGEROW: last Essays. With Portrait. Crown 8vo., 3s. 6d.
  THE STORY OF MY HEART: my Autobiography. With Portrait and New Preface by C. J. LONGMAN. Crown 8vo., 3s. 6d.
  RED DEER. With 17 Illustrations by J. CHARLTON and H. TUNALY. Crown 8vo., 3s. 6d.
  THE TOILERS OF THE FIELD. With Portrait from the Bust in Salisbury Cathedral. Crown 8vo., 6s.
  WOOD MAGIC: a Fable. With Vignette by E. V. B. Crown 8vo., 3s. 6d.

Jewsbury.—SELECTIONS FROM THE LETTERS OF GERALDINE ENDSOR JEWSBURY TO JANE WELSH CARLYLE. Edited by Mrs. ALEXANDER IRELAND. 8vo.,16s.

Johnson.—THE PATENTEE'S MANUAL: a Treatise on the Law and Practice of Letters Patent. By J. & J. H. JOHNSON, Patent Agents, &c. 8vo., 10s. 6d.

Lang.—Works by ANDREW LANG.
  LETTERS TO DEAD AUTHORS. Fcp. 8vo., 2s. 6d. net.
  BOOKS AND BOOKMEN. With 2 Coloured Plates and 17 Illustrations. Fcp. 8vo., 2s. 6d. net.
  OLD FRIENDS. Fcp. 8vo., 2s. 6d. net.
  LETTERS ON LITERATURE. Fcp. 8vo., 2s. 6d. net.

Macfarren.—LECTURES ON HARMONY. By Sir GEO. A. MACFARREN. 8vo., 12s.

Matthews.—PEN AND INK: Papers on Subjects of more or less importance. By BRANDER MATTHEWS. Crown 8vo., 5s.

Max Müller.—Works by F. MAX MÜLLER.
  HIBBERT LECTURES ON THE ORIGIN AND GROWTH OF RELIGION, as illustrated by the Religions of India. Crown 8vo., 7s. 6d. [*continued.*

Max Müller.—Works by F. MAX MÜLLER.—*continued.*
  INTRODUCTION TO THE SCIENCE OF RELIGION: Four Lectures delivered at the Royal Institution. Cr. 8vo., 3s. 6d.
  NATURAL RELIGION. The Gifford Lectures, 1888. Cr. 8vo., 10s. 6d.
  PHYSICAL RELIGION. The Gifford Lectures, 1890. Cr. 8vo., 10s. 6d.
  ANTHROPOLOGICAL RELIGION. The Gifford Lectures, 1891. Cr. 8vo., 10s. 6d.
  THEOSOPHY OR PSYCHOLOGICAL RELIGION. The Gifford Lectures, 1892. Cr. 8vo., 10s. 6d.
  INDIA: WHAT CAN IT TEACH US? Cr. 8vo., 3s. 6d.

Mendelssohn.—THE LETTERS OF FELIX MENDELSSOHN. Translated by Lady WALLACE. 2 vols. Cr. 8vo., 10s.

Milner.—COUNTRY PLEASURES: the Chronicle of a Year chiefly in a Garden. By GEORGE MILNER. Cr. 8vo., 3s. 6d.

Perring.—HARD KNOTS IN SHAKESPEARE. By Sir PHILIP PERRING, Bart. 8vo., 7s. 6d.

Proctor.—Works by RICHARD A. PROCTOR.
  STRENGTH AND HAPPINESS. With 9 Illustrations. Crown 8vo., 5s.
  STRENGTH: How to get Strong and keep Strong, with Chapters on Rowing and Swimming, Fat, Age, and the Waist. With 9 Illus. Cr. 8vo., 2s.

Richardson.—NATIONAL HEALTH. A Review of the Works of Sir Edwd. Chadwick, K.C.B. By Sir B. W. RICHARDSON, M.D. Cr., 4s. 6d.

Roget.—A HISTORY OF THE 'OLD WATER-COLOUR SOCIETY' (now the Royal Society of Painters in Water-Colours). By JOHN LEWIS ROGET. 2 vols. Royal 8vo., 42s.

Rossetti.—A SHADOW OF DANTE: being an Essay towards studying Himself, his World, and his Pilgrimage. By MARIA FRANCESCA ROSSETTI. With Illustrations and design on cover by DANTE GABRIEL ROSSETTI. Cr. 8vo., 10s. 6d.

Southey.—CORRESPONDENCE WITH CAROLINE BOWLES. By ROBERT SOUTHEY. Edited by E. DOWDEN. 8vo., 14s.

Wallaschek.—PRIMITIVE MUSIC: an Inquiry into the Origin and Development of Music, Songs, Instruments, Dances, and Pantomimes of Savage Races. By RICHARD WALLASCHEK. With Musical Examples. 8vo., 12s. 6d.

www.ingramcontent.com/pod-product-compliance
Lightning Source LLC
Chambersburg PA
CBHW032120230426
43672CB00009B/1809